If I had my life to live over

I would pick more daisies

Edited by Sandra Haldeman Martz

papier-mache

Papier-Mache Press
Watsonville CA

Other anthologies edited by Sandra Haldeman Martz

When I Am an Old Woman I Shall Wear Purple
If I Had a Hammer: Women's Work
The Tie That Binds

If I Had My Life to Live Over
I Would Pick More Daisies

Edited by Sandra Haldeman Martz
Papier-Mache Press
Watsonville, California

ISBN: 0-918949-24-6 Softcover
ISBN: 0-918949-25-4 Hardcover

Edited by Sandra Haldeman Martz
Cover art, "More," fabric and thread, Copyright © 1992 by Deidre Scherer
Cover design by Cynthia Heier

Grateful acknowledgment is made to the following publications which first published some of the material in this book:

Passages North, vol. 3, no. 2, Spring/Summer 1982 and *A Decade of Good Writing, Passages North Anthology* (Milkweed Editions) © 1990 for "Old Friend Sends a Chain Letter" by Therese Becker; *Common Touch*, vol. 2, no. 2, Spring 1992, © 1992 The Straub Association for "Life Support" by Dorothy Howe Brooks; *Kinnikinnik*, vol. 1, no. 5, December 1990 for "Small Life" by Lizabeth Carpenter; *Phoebe*, vol. 3, no. 1, Spring 1991 for "Broken Vows" by Joan Connor; *Bluff City*, vol. 3, no. 1 © 1992 for "It Is Enough" by Ruth Daigon; *Spectrum* for "If I Could Begin Again" by Sue Saniel Elkind; *The Torch*, August 1991 for "Eating Cantaloupe" by Midge Farmer; *North Dakota Quarterly*, vol. 59, no. 1, Winter 1991 for "On Loving a Younger Man" by Alice Friman; *Bachy*, vol. 15, Fall 1979 and *My Self In Another Skin* (Drenan Press) 1981 for "A Palsied Girl Goes to the Beach" by Nan Hunt; *Poetry* vol. CLX, no. 3, June 1992, © 1992 The Modern Poetry Association for "Adoption" by Alison Kolodinsky; *Midwest Poetry Review* vol. VII, no. 2, 1986, and *Catching the Light* (Pocahontas Press, Inc.) 1989 for "Counterpoint" by Lynn Kozma; *Open City*, no. 257 (1984) and *Pudding Magazine*, no. 15 (1987) for "Vietnam" by Jennifer Lagier; *The Vincent Brothers Review*, vol. IV, no. 3, issue #10 for "The Scorpion Wore Pink Shoes" by Janice Levy; *Crosscurrents*, vol. 10, no. 2, Spring 1992 for "Ripening" by Joanne McCarthy; *Tucumcari Literary Review*, August 1990 for a different form of "The Sacrifice" by Shirley Vogler Meister; *February Caprice* 1991 for "Art As Life" by Ann Menebroker; *The Cooke Book: A Seasoning of Poets* (SCOP Publications) 1988 for "A Woman's Choice" by Jacklyn W. Potter; *Ita* (Capricorn Publishing Pty, Ltd) © 1990, 1991 and *Fair Lady* (National Magazines) © 1990, 1991, 1992 for "Cauliflower Beach" by Carol Schwalberg; *Morning of the Red-Tailed Hawk* (Green River Press) © 1981 for "October Fire" by Bettie M. Sellers; *The Montana Review* and *Stalking the Florida Panther* (The Word Works) 1988 for "The Keeper of Spaces" by Enid Shomer; and *Nebo: A Literary Journal*, vol. 8, no. 1 and 2, Fall/Spring 1989-90 and *Tucumcari Literary Review*, vol. III, no. 1, issue 13, January/February 1990 for "Mother Land" by Linda Wasmer Smith.

Library of Congress Cataloging-in-Publication Data

If I had my life to live over, I would pick more daisies / edited by
   Sandra Haldeman Martz.
      p.   cm.
      ISBN 0-918949-24-6 (pbk.) : $10.00.—ISBN 0-918949-25-4 : $16.00
      1. Women—United States—Literary collections.   2. American
literature—Women authors.   3. American literature—20th century.
I. Martz, Sandra.
PS509.W6I4   1992
810.8'09287—dc20   92-34059
                                                                                                              CIP

To the women who inspired me to make wiser choices
and the women who comforted me when I made foolish ones.

Contents

Foreword

If I had my life to live over...

At some time almost everyone has reflected on life's crossroads and wondered what the outcome would have been had we chosen different paths. Especially when viewed from our later years, we often feel a sense of having sacrificed some of the quality of life in order to achieve material goals or in some other way meet public expectations.

It is in that horizon of our imagination—where the unlimited possibilities of "what might have been" form a background against which our understanding of "what is" emerges—that we find the universal appeal of this anthology and its title piece, "If I Had My Life to Live Over." The version included here is attributed to Nadine Stair, an eighty-five-year-old woman from Louisville, Kentucky, but the work can be found in many forms and often with no ascribed author. This small prose piece, with its commitment to a fuller life, a life with "more ice cream and less beans," has inspired many to pen their own visions of a life relived. It thus provides the perfect starting place for a word journey through women's experiences, exploring the spectrum of women's choices.

With poems, stories, and photographs chosen from more than 3,000 manuscripts received over a two-year period, *If I Had My Life to Live Over I Would Pick More Daisies* moves from childhood to adulthood through old age, reminding us that our options are both limited and extended by personal belief systems, ethnic and cultural identity, class and economic status, age, and gender.

Our choices are seldom simple or straightforward: right or wrong, yes or no. They are more often complex and conflictive and intertwined with the decisions made by others. And while the larger, more public choices such as education or career paths or political activism may have the more obvious impact on our lives, it is often those small private moments of decision, known only to ourselves, that live vividly in our memories. It is this latter group of choices that constitutes the core of this collection. My hope is that this book will touch the hearts of readers as it has touched mine.

SANDRA HALDEMAN MARTZ

IF I HAD MY LIFE TO LIVE OVER
I WOULD PICK MORE DAISIES

Photo by Lori Burkhalter-Lackey

If I Had My Life to Live Over

Nadine Stair

I'd dare to make more mistakes next time. I'd relax, I would limber up. I would be sillier than I have been this trip. I would take fewer things seriously. I would take more chances. I would climb more mountains and swim more rivers. I would eat more ice cream and less beans. I would perhaps have more actual troubles, but I'd have fewer imaginary ones.

You see, I'm one of those people who live sensibly and sanely hour after hour, day after day. Oh, I've had my moments, and if I had it to do over again, I'd have more of them. In fact, I'd try to have nothing else. Just moments, one after another, instead of living so many years ahead of each day. I've been one of those persons who never goes anywhere without a thermometer, a hot water bottle, a raincoat and a parachute. If I had to do it again, I would travel lighter than I have.

If I had my life to live over, I would start barefoot earlier in the spring and stay that way later in the fall. I would go to more dances. I would ride more merry-go-rounds. I would pick more daisies.

Requiem

Martha B. Jordan

For Angel Camacho

When the last from childhood dies
the heartbeat slows
to a dry leaf rustle
no one calls you
niña
and
tu
or whispers charms
like river water rushing
over moss
and fish
and pebbles
sana, sana, colita de rana.

Loving Jerry

Jan Epton Seale

I have been wondering since the second grade what it feels like to fall in love. Then I get the note on Monday: MEET ME AT RECESS BY THE WATER FOUNTING.

Jerry McCondle is one of the few people, boys or girls, in the whole fourth grade that fills up his T-shirt. (My mother says, "Nelda, you are so-o-o scrawny," when she pins me into a dress she is sewing for me.)

The other boys have sharp, bony shoulders and their T-shirts hang on them in wrinkles, showing their mothers have not flapped them before hanging them on the clothesline. (One time when my mother made me wear a shirt a little bit wrinkled, I cried. She said, "Nelda, only real pretty girls have to have everything perfect.")

Anyway, Jerry's shirt even looks bulgy. And his jeans make a soft, swishing sound when he comes up the aisle.

He drops the little triangle-folded note in my lap as he comes back from collecting last Friday's spelling test. I leave it there and take off my glasses, holding them up like I'm wondering if they need cleaning. If I hold them a certain way, they are like a mirror, and I can see Jerry behind me wadding his spelling test into a little ball and chucking it into his inkwell.

At the fountain, Jerry is careful to be five people ahead of me. He waits beside the water, saying things to each kid in line, sometimes slapping the water up into a person's face, especially if they are wearing glasses.

When my turn comes, I try to wipe my mouth before I raise my head but the icy water makes my lips numb and I can't tell whether I've gotten them dry when I raise up. In a way, I hope I haven't. The models in my mother's magazines all have wet lips.

"Hi," I say, feeling silly because I've been in the same room with him all morning. He doesn't splash my glasses and that makes me wonder if he is in love with me. He turns and walks beside me, not saying a word, just looking out at the baseball diamond where Rosemary and John are choosing their teams.

We stop behind the backstop. "We're going to sit there," he says, pointing to the old bleachers.

When we are settled, Jerry holds out his arm. On the inside is a big blue heart that looks a little like the beautiful tattoo my Uncle Charles came home from the war with. It could be from the blue pen we have to use for English. The arrow could be from our red arithmetic correction pen. How would I know?

"Nelda," Jerry says slowly, "on Friday I'm going to have them put a girl's name in this. On Friday."

"That's nice," I say, staring out on the field where nothing much is going on yet. I figure I should probably know who "them" is.

When we go back inside, the health lesson is on the alimentary canal, and my best friend Maydean and I glance through the chapter and count *body* four times and *bowel* twice. (Maydean has been in love I don't know how many times since last year when she moved to our school.)

Of course, the teacher calls on me to read aloud. She always calls on me. One of my paragraphs says *body*, and it makes me so nervous I start grinning when I get to that line, and by the time I get to the word, I laugh out loud, put my hand over my mouth, and start coughing. Across the aisle, Maydean clamps her hand over her mouth too.

Miss Schumaker stands and stares at us. "May I ask what is so funny?"

I shake my head and continue to cough. There is no way to tell Miss Schumaker that Maydean and I *know* that *body* is a nasty word.

Tuesday morning Jerry is waiting for me when I come up the walk. His hair is parted a little crooked but it is all combed with Vitalis. I check whether his heart has washed off. It is there, and I'm still thinking about whether he took a bath last night and redid the heart, or whether he did not take a bath at all, just put on a clean shirt, when he speaks to me.

"Meet me again today, same place," Jerry says as we pass into the front hall where Mr. Jenkins, the principal, is standing in a brown suit with his arms folded.

"Shhh!" I say.

Jerry glances back at Mr. Jenkins. "To hell with him," Jerry says, but quietly and right in my ear.

Maydean writes me a note during lunch-count: DO YOU LOVE JERRY? YES _____ NO _____ .

Before I can answer back, the teacher starts the six-weeks spelling review. I put Maydean's note in my desk.

Before recess, I check my socks, that the backs of them have not worked down inside my shoes. Jerry is waiting for me, and we walk out to the bleachers again.

"Yep, Friday," Jerry says when we're settled. He's looking at his heart. He digs in his pants pocket and offers me a stick of Juicy Fruit. I say, "Thanks," and unwrap it slowly, thinking about what I might make out of the foil. Jerry takes two pieces for himself, unwraps them, rolls them together, says "Watch," and throws them in his mouth like popcorn.

We stare out at Rosemary and John's teams, who are playing for real today. Once, I forget and clap and scream "Yea!" when Sharon hits the ball into right field.

She throws down the bat and runs to first base. "She's deader 'n a doornail," Jerry says. "Shit! Ten to one, they've got 'er."

I'm thinking whether Jerry should have said that to me when he scoots a little closer. I have my hand on the seat, with my skirt spread over it, and now he runs in his hand and gets hold of mine. His hand feels real warm and rough and a little wet. The wet part surprises me. I look back toward the building, checking if Miss Schumaker might be looking at us out the window.

Now we sit staring at the ball game. Jerry is concentrating, you might say. But I am trying to memorize everything about Jerry's hand to check out with Maydean later. Am I holding it too tight or too loose? Suddenly, Jerry doubles back his middle finger and starts rubbing it slowly inside my hand.

I look at Jerry. He is looking extra hard at the ball field, his eyes kind of scrunched. I think he must have seen something awful and I look. Nobody is even up to bat.

On Wednesday it rains in the morning so we stay inside. When that happens, the girls play jacks in the corners of the room and the boys play rubber horseshoes in the hall.

Jerry waits for me after school, and we ride our bicycles side by side until Bluebonnet Grocery, where he fishes in his pocket for two dimes, tells me to stay with the bikes, goes in, and comes out with two Grapettes. We drink them there under the dripping trees. I try not to get any around my mouth. Jerry fits his lips inside the bottle on purpose.

So his whole mouth is purple. "Want a kiss?" he asks and smacks me before I can decide for myself.

"Je-e-rry!" I say, like I know I'm supposed to, and turn away. He laughs and carries the bottles back in.

When I get home, Mother asks me why I'm late. "I had to go back and get my speller." I am careful not to open my mouth too wide. I race through the house to the bathroom. Anyway, the speller is partly the truth.

Thursday when Jerry goes to the board to diagram the sentence Miss Schumaker has assigned him, he drops another note in my lap. When Miss Schumaker gets all mad because Jerry has put an adjective on the subject line, I open the note. It has I LOVE NELDA written a billion times on it, from one corner sideways, over and over, to the bottom. At the end it says, IF I DECIDE THEY RITE YOUR NAME ON MY ARM, YOU GET ONE OF THESE EVER DAY AFTER THAT—FOREVER.

I refold the note and put it in my desk. I take off my glasses and fold them. I cross my arms and lay my head on them. It seems like all I am doing is folding things. I am too tired. I roll my head and pick out Jerry at the board.

He is all fuzzy around the edges but I can still see that some of his hair has gotten loose and is sticking straight up in back. I begin to think how my mother calls a cowlick a turkey tail, and which name is right.

Jerry is erasing his sentence after Miss Schumaker has told him to start over and do it right this time. He's not erasing neatly. He's doing it like swipe! swipe! making puffs of chalk dust. I squint and try to see the heart on his arm, but I can't. I don't know if it's because he's moving his arm too fast or because I don't have on my glasses.

I raise up and reach inside my desk. I feel Maydean's note and bring it out. I press it out on my desk and uncap my pen. I check NO.

Small Life

Lizabeth Carpenter

It was March first. Outside the land thawed imperceptibly under harsh easterly winds blowing over the plains.

Lakota City lies along the Big Yellow River, on the alluvial plain south of Granite and Larchwood. In the spring, if you hike the river's muddy banks downstream, through its wild westward thrusts and counter curves to the east, you'll need insect repellent and long pants—the soil of the floodplain breeds gnats, chiggers, hornets, ticks, cockleburs, snakes. Every other decade a bull moose is sighted far from its native mountain rangeland, thrashing through cattails and cornfields, lumbering across Highway Five. But this is the exception; most of life here, in its abundance, is small and unnoticeable, deceivingly safe.

Marly left school at noon. Chunks of ice floated on the river, its steep clay banks soft and treacherous, patterned with tiny bird prints. She stepped carefully on matted wet leaves at the top of the bank. Wiry shrubs poked her hands and sides and slapped against her face. She progressed slowly. She climbed up one side of an eroded ditch with her hands braced against the muscle over each knee—"knobby knees," Clayton called them—and stumbled at the top over half-buried timber. Last night she and Clayton had parked on War Eagle's Bluff and opened all the car windows to the warm spring breeze. When they'd kissed, he had touched her knobby knee under her skirt. His hand was trembling; she became very still. Her instincts had abandoned her. The city glowed blue-white on the southern horizon as a slow warm river crept through her legs and arms and chest. The car was quiet except for their breathing, the rustle of clothing, leather seats.

Suddenly, fiercely, she pushed him away.

Clayton rested a moment against the steering wheel. "Blocked shot," he said. He laughed shortly, started up the Beetle, and drove Marly home.

Remembering this, Marly froze again, her hand gripping a thin willow tree. Behind her, upriver, five bridge supports like huge cement doorways stood spaced across the water, awaiting construction of a new state highway. Between here and the city it seemed pastures vanished monthly, the land slipping away like snowmelt, sprouting boxy new prefab or brick-fronted homes.

A warm wind pushed through the leafless branches and lifted the hair off Marly's forehead—the air so dry and clean, so settling, she was afraid to imagine a world without such untouched lonely places. She didn't know how she would live.

Broken Vows

Joan Connor

I stand before the mirror in the chapel hall, fidgeting with the chin strap of my veil. I see my parents behind me, reversed in the mirror. I have a queasy feeling, like car sickness, as if I were traveling backward. The floral scent of my bouquet—of the flower arrangements, the lilies and glads and roses—intermingle, heady and cloying. The chin strap cuts into my neck. The images in the mirror blur, and a memory surfaces, entire.

Summer vacation. I can smell Mom's perfume and some peanuts she is munching. I slide the bead on my hat strap up to my chin. We crossed the California state-line six road signs and at least that many backseat tussles ago. Kyle and Jamie are scrapping their way cross-country. The scuffle picked up in Minnesota when Jamie drew the battle lines right down his third of the backseat, using the khaki strap of his canteen for a marker. Outside Minneapolis, I moved out of the front lines into the front seat between Mom and Dad. Jamie nudged the canteen strap into the center of the backseat, and he and Kyle have been at each other ever since. Today is particularly bad. Dad has warned them to cut it out four times. His knuckles look almost blue against the shiny black of the steering wheel. Dad is humming, but the hum sounds tight, forced. I try to ignore Kyle and Jamie, train my eyes on the road ahead, but the road here pushes itself on like a drudge through a round of chores. No roadside distractions. Only great over-arching trees and their shadows.

Sometimes Dad and I sing to drown out the boys. I love it when Dad sings to me, slightly off-key and very deep. My favorite is the song he's humming now, "Clementine." The hum breaks into words. "Dwelt a miner, forty-niner, and his daughter Clementine. Oh, my darling," he wails, "Oh, my darling."

Mom taps out the time or her impatience on the dashboard.

"Oh, my darling, Clementine" I join in, high and sweet. I tug the brim of my Deadwood cowboy hat over my eyes. Dad bought me the hat, red with white embroidery, in South Dakota. I love it. In Yellowstone, the hat blew off and landed on the crusty edge of a bubbling hot mudpot, two yards out, just far enough so that my father couldn't reach it. While I cried and my mother screamed, my father hopped the boardwalk fence, tiptoed past the Danger sign, and retrieved the hat. You've got to harmonize with someone who would do that for you. I chime in as Dad starts, "You are lost...," but the boys' voices cut the song short.

"It's mine," Kyle wails in a pitch that crawls up my spine.

"That's it," Dad yells. "Enough. I've had enough."

The boys lurch forward in midsquabble as Dad jumps on the brake.

"I asked you to stop bickering half a state ago. Now get out. Get out of my car." His voice surprisingly soft, he thumps the steering wheel as he speaks.

"Duncan," my mother protests, "they've been cooped up in the car all day."

"Then uncoop," Dad answers her. His eyes sight the length of the car's hood like a gun barrel. "All I asked for was a little peace while I drove. I just asked you to keep them quiet. So uncoop," he repeats, and adds, "now."

"But Jamie crossed the line," Kyle whines. "He started it. He put his tomahawk on my side of the seat. See?" Kyle asks. "Look."

I tip my hat back off my head and twist in my seat to examine the evidence.

"I don't want to hear it, not one whine of it, not one explanation. Just get out of the damn car," Dad says.

"But there's nothing here," Mom says, scanning the area, "just a rest stop." Dad does not even turn to look at her. She sighs. Without another word, she yanks the handle on the passenger side. The boys tumble out, grumbling. I start scooting across the seat toward the open door, but Dad touches my forearm. "Except you, Molly," he says, turning. "You can stay if you want. You weren't in it."

I stare at my father's blue eyes. They waver, hazy, like car metal, hot in the sun. I hear Kyle behind me, whining, "It isn't fair," as Mom shoos the boys away from the Galaxie. My hat cord cuts into my neck. My chest tightens. I glance at Mom and Jamie and Kyle standing on the shoulder of the highway. I look back at my father's eyes and consider this offer. I blush.

"Go or stay, Molly," my dad says, "but make up your mind now." He turns his attention back to the hood of the Galaxie.

The sun bounces off the windshield, stunning me. I cannot see my father's face in the glare. My heart bangs in my left side, the side close to my father, the side that wants to remain on the seat. My right arm lifts and reaches toward the passenger door, the handle. My right hand hovers there. The moment suspends itself. How can he make me choose? Then Kyle whimpers. Ready to cry myself, and without realizing that I have made a choice, I reject my father. The vinyl seat smooches the hot backs of my thighs as I inch across the seat to the door. I slam the door shut. I want to whisper, "I love you, Daddy." But the Galaxie squeals off. Mom stares at the rear license plate as it recedes, her eyes following the Galaxie to the vanishing point.

"Wow. Look at the patch of rubber Dad laid, Mom." Jamie admires the tire marks, parallel black zippers, a shade darker than the tarmac.

But Mom does not respond. Her face composes itself in some expression that is almost no expression, drying like papier-mâché into a mask. "Come on. Let's cross the street." She takes Jamie's and Kyle's hands and guides them across the highway as if she were stemming traffic. But the road stretches empty and quiet like a road nobody lives on, a road whose only purpose is to connect at either end with other roads.

"You really done it now," Jamie says, craning around Mom's leg for a shot at Kyle. "Dad's gone off and left us for good."

"No sir," Kyle says. "No sir. You did it, James Patrick. I told you to keep your junk on your side of the car. Didn't I tell him to keep his junk on his side of the car?" Kyle asks looking up at my mother.

"Stop bickering," Mom says and tightens their wrists in her bracelets of fingers.

"Ouch. Stop it. You're hurting me." Jamie tugs, but Mom keeps walking across the road. As I follow them, my hat thuds rhythmically between my shoulder blades. In the rest stop on the other side, some picnic tables rot in the shadows of the giant firs. Mom releases the boys, drops her shoulder bag on a bench, and sits in a mound of pine needles at the base of the tree. Jamie inspects some graffiti carved in the table top. Kyle slumps against a trash barrel, curling up very small. "Is he coming back?" Kyle asks my mother.

"Yes," my mom says, "he's coming back." She trickles some pine needles into the palm of her hand, lets them sift through her fingers. I wonder how she knows Dad is coming back, how she can be so sure. But when she raises her eyes, they meet mine, patient and certain.

"When?" Kyle asks.

"When he's ready," she says.

"Today?"

Mom shrugs. "I think probably." Her lips curve into the merest smile.

"Where'd he go?" Kyle asks.

"Who cares? Stop being such a baby," Jamie says.

"I imagine he went to see the sequoias," Mom answers Kyle, talking over Jamie. "Your father's wanted to make this camping trip, coast to coast, since he was a boy himself."

"Good going, Jamie," Kyle says. "Now we'll never see the sequoias; will we, Mom?"

"Shut up," Jamie says.

"Yeah, shut up, Jamie," I second.

"You," Jamie sneers. "You should have gone with him. Daddy's widdle girlie-whirlie."

"Yeah, well maybe I should have," I say. I pick a prickly pine needle from my ankle sock.

"Stop bickering," Mom says, but the command has no air in it. Her voice sounds tired as she asks, "Don't you kids ever learn? Why do you think we are sitting here on the side of the road?"

Kyle flops down on the ground in a sulk. Jamie lies on his stomach on the picnic table, tracing anonymous monograms with his fingers. "Anybody got a knife?" he asks, but no one bothers to answer him. I sit next to Mom and watch her nudge the pine needles into ridges, mound them into mountains.

"What if he doesn't come back?" Kyle asks.

"He'll come back," Mom says. She rubs a smutch of pitch from her forefinger with her thumb.

"What are the sequoias like, Mom?" Jamie asks.

"I've never seen them," she says, tilting her head back against the tree trunk. "But I imagine they're like this. Only bigger. Bigger and older."

We all look up through the tree branches, higher than anything we could have imagined back home in Maine. The morning becomes afternoon, golden and dusty. Jamie and Kyle build castles in the pine needles. When Kyle grows cranky and hungry, Mom scrounges around in her pocketbook, producing three sticks of Juicy Fruit, a few peanuts, and some restaurant packets of saltines. The crackers are dry and gum my tongue like communion wafers. Mom rests. Kyle falls asleep with his head on her leg. Jamie complains. We pretend not to be listening for cars until a drone small as a bee's grows louder, more mechanical as it nears. Jamie twitches, then leaps up yelling, "I knew he'd come back. I knew it." But the drone precedes a truck, loaded with scabby logs, its claw clanking on its crane as it passes. The roar recedes, and Jamie's face reddens. But he won't let himself cry; he's twelve-and-a-half years old. "Made ya look," he mutters as he sprawls on the ground.

Later, when I cry, Mom finds a packet of tissues in her purse. She comforts me as she pats my back. "Your dad's just tired of camping, sleeping on the ground, driving all day, being cooped up in the car. He just needs a break. Time and space to walk around for a while. Away from us," she says.

I recognize the truth of these explanations. We've been camping cross-country since June. But I'm not crying because I'm on the side of the road in a place that has no name or traffic. I'm crying because I chose, and nothing will ever be the same again, because I looked into my father's urgent blue eyes, eyes so near to mine that I can almost see his world through them, and I turned away from them for two boys sniveling in red crew cuts, boys most of the time I don't even like very much, and a woman in a faded madras skirt. Like "The Farmer in the Dell," I stepped inside the family circle while my father, the last, unchosen player, stood like the cheese at the song's end, alone.

This is what I try to tell my mother as I cry, but the words garble themselves. She hushes me. I think she does not understand. But her palm on my cheek hesitates with an almost imperceptible impatience as if, here in this stand of secretive old trees, she understands the choice perfectly, completely, and can just barely restrain herself from hastening the moment along.

"Stop your blubbering," Jamie says, and he butts my shoulder, one of his rough comforts. He flushes when I smile at him. Mom eases me off her shoulder.

I sit upright and wonder how we must look to a stranger driving by, a misplaced family of four, unwashed and unfed, huddled at the roots of these titanic evergreens. We must look stunted. Small. Observed by this strange eye, I let the fancy draw me in, pretending we are characters illustrating the frontispiece of an old wives' tale.

We listen to the wind stir as the day dims. Dusky, we huddle around the table. Small stars spin out, pinwheeling orphans. Out of time and place. My mother, my brothers, and I sit on the damp benches. A meager congregation. Is this the image the Galaxie's headlights catch in the beams of my father's memory?

When we clamber, sleepy and sheepish, into the car, my father does not apologize. And my mother asks him no questions. But we do not go to a campground. We spend the night at a Holiday Inn. My father brings paper sacks of hamburgers to the room. And he does not complain when Jamie and Kyle tussle and tumble on their rollaways or turn the hotel TV up too loud.

But I have trouble falling asleep, listening to my mother's breath keeping time with my father's. When I close my eyes, the floor of my dream collapses. I fall through. Everything skews. I land, wholly awake, in an old, known place, but I am totally new.

In a few years, "Remember the sequoias" will become a family joke, the wry alarm Dad sounds when Jamie won't say where he's going or when he expects to be back, when Kyle won't submit to a haircut, when I take too long picking out a dress for church, when Mom's defense of our misdeeds becomes too strident. "Remember the sequoias," the reminder that family ties can stretch to the snapping point, transforms itself into a unifying anecdote, a family rallying cry. Our in-joke. Kyle, Jamie, and my mother learn to laugh with my father, but I cringe. My memory differs from theirs: Dad ordered them from the car, but I decided to go. Worlds tilted at that decision. I declined the man, the pull of his gravity, wobbled away and aligned myself in a safe system of familial orbit. I don't know if he ever realized the scope of that choice, or its repercussions. I do not know if, in that instant, I hurt him, and, if I did, if he recalls it. But I changed forever. I realized that life entailed a series of compromises of the private self to the public, a slow accommodation to ordinariness, to convention's momentum. I had vowed to resist being trundled along by the ongoingness of life. But I did not. I do not.

I make this coward's choice again on my wedding, fidgeting before the mirror, knowing that at the end of the aisle a man my father doesn't like, but at least doesn't hate, waits for me. The memory subsides. My father's face attends me, pale, almost blank, as if he'd like to be somewhere, anywhere, else. Maybe in a Galaxie, alone and racing against the clock.

On the periphery of my vision, I spot my mother, trumped up in a silly blue-lace gown. Her face, pink and happy, stings me as I understand for the first time her joy today and her patience as she sat on roadsides for twenty years, certain that my father would always return but that I one day would stand in this corner with my father about to usher me off. I startle at the nearness of my father's face and realize he is speaking to me.

"Remember the sequoias," he says.

My mother laughs abruptly and too loudly. Tears sting my nose, pungent, piney. The phrase has been a family adage for years; it shouldn't surprise me now. But it does.

"Don't worry, honey," he says to my startled face. "Your old man wouldn't desert you now." Clumsily, he kisses my cheek. "You made the right choice," he whispers.

I wonder which choice he means; which choice, judicious, stands alone. But in an instant all the choices blur, seem one long attenuated and inevitable choice I've been making all my life. I close my eyes on my confusion, and I see a shower of shooting stars on the dark domes of my eyelids. All the scenery I missed that summer unrolling beyond the Galaxie window, while I, nearsighted, looked in the wrong direction, unreels in tangles on the floor. I wonder what became of my Deadwood hat, what trash can I stuffed it into, what friend's house I left it at, what carton, what moving van I failed to pack it in.

"It's time," my mother says as the organ cues us. And my father wheels me around and guides me down the aisle. The walk stretches long and empty as if its only purpose is to connect one point of departure with the next. My feet choose the way, and every step, every choice is an exclusion of possibility, a diminution of the boundless self. I'm dressed in white, a flutter of lace and satin ribbons, glittering like the votive candles in a liar's eyes. At the end of the aisle a man in black tails waits.

A Palsied Girl Goes to the Beach

Nan Hunt

Empty now of voices except
my duplicating hum of loneliness
my room is airless; and I crab-crawl
my way downstairs where
children, their questions raw and
open, stare at my praying mantis-stance.
But the adults snap to attention
shift and shadow out of reach.

I would clutch them back
just to fence the cruelty.
My mind must put the lid
on their revulsion (clambering inside
like spiders under glass)
their dread that between us lies
fate's mere flirting finger-snap.

Each step of mine is a tightrope test.
The signal to the muscle shoots
a devious, interrupted race
and when my foot sways down
my will must   stalk it
until it comes to place.
Jerk and twitch   I get there.

I offer my dangled limbs
for the sun's hot benediction
fingering shells as rosaries
for the dear struggles wet

in living things.
And, braced against the curling surf
I, inconsequential as coquinas
scoured over, stay the waves.

And more than stay—
resist.

Photo by Marianne Gontarz

The Keeper of Spaces

Enid Shomer

I am the keeper of usually
vacant spaces. I am the one
who notes how bare the swamp oak grows
as it opens its arms to the wind
in early fall. I notch
the southern skies with gray
before the migratory birds
fly past.

It is not voids
but possibilities I see:
the ribbed hull of a leaf
where tea scale gains
its barnacle grip,
the scalloped calyx cup
where mites drink dry
the bloom.

I am the one who, looking
at my hand, sees not a shape
but all the places
where the hand must go,
and the spaces between fingers
where life like sand escapes
even as I make
a fist.

Adoption

Alison Kolodinsky

I stitched us together by night
in the rocking chair, marveled
at your fingers, the foreign navel,
memorized the sweep of your eyebrows,
unraveled your language.
Having accepted the unfamiliar,
I kept watch
for proof of our union.

Tonight I inhale as I kiss
your perfect face, moist
from busy dreaming. Your fragrance
marks me—that fingerprint
only a parent can read.
I crawl in beside you, grateful
and patient, to dip us
with even breath
in this night's ink.

Photo by Anna Tomczak

The Sacrifice

Shirley Vogler Meister

A child is growing somewhere
    in this weary world,
    an innocent unwary
    of emotions shattered,
    a child whose life around
    mute hearts is curled,
    who'll never know how much
    his being mattered.
Lovingly, she chose to yield
    at birth the son
    she bore with courage
    in her unwed prime.
    Clearly, she saw
    paternal lack of worth
    as parent or as spouse:
    poor paradigm.
Reality pressed close
    and she perceived
    how only hope
    was left to give her son,
    that good intent would not
    their needs relieve:
    the sacrificial web
    was firmly spun.

Adoptive keepers now
    assume his care
    and fill his time
    with wonders far removed
    from lineal love
    that evermore still dares
    to grow—a selfless love
    already proved.

Photo by Marianne Gontarz

Holy Places

Stephany Brown

Oh, honey, don't hurt me. I'm too old. This is what my mother used to say to me all the time when I reached the age when girls become smart-alecky to their mothers. I realize now that she wasn't old then, just prematurely gray. "Early silver," my father used to say as he held on to a hunk of her waist-length hair. But it worked. I wasn't unkind to her like my friend Sally was to her solidly brunette mother and Anne-Marie to hers. I figured Mom just couldn't take it, the old being more fragile than the young.

And she wasn't unkind to me either, even when I broke all the rules and got pregnant at sixteen. I should have been smart enough to figure out that if she could handle an out-of-wedlock baby, she could handle an unkind word or two. But by that time I'd lost the urge to be smart-alecky. I had other things on my mind.

Mainly Jeff. Jeff in his white Spitfire, one hand on the steering wheel, the other somewhere on me. He'd turn on the Motown station and if the top was down and we were on a country road he'd turn the music up loud and sing along with the Four Tops or Mary Wells or Smoky Robinson and the Miracles. When we reached our cornfield, all the sounds would stop, and it would seem for a minute that we'd entered a church. And after a time the cornfield always seemed like a holy place to us, even if there hadn't been any noise on the way there.

It wasn't our cornfield, though, neither his nor mine. It was almost an hour away from our neighborhood and it was farmed by people we never saw. We only went there at night. Jeff loved the drive there, the long straight road lined with tall trees and farms. When the night was bright enough we could see the outlines of old silos. He'd go way too fast, seventy-five or eighty, but I didn't have the heart to tell him I was scared.

Sometimes there'd be straw in my hair when I got home. My mother, who'd have been reading on the couch or playing back-gammon with my father, would pick some of it out and say that I'd missed curfew again, that she couldn't help worrying when I was late. "And that little car is so flimsy," she'd say, "it would protect you no more than a tuna fish can; what if a truck hits you?" I told her once that Jeff was saving up for a Cadillac that would protect us, but I said it nicely, the old being unable to handle sarcasm.

My sweet father, for the most part, stayed out of these conversations. Sometimes he would nod and say, "Your mother's right, honey," or echo something she had said. He figured it was some mother-daughter thing. Or he figured sex was involved. Or maybe he just saw my mother as wiser than he.

She was wise. She knew I was pregnant before I did and before any test had been done. She could tell by my face, she said, by the way it puffed out a little. I was horrified and expected her to be mad but she said she knew I loved Jeff and that Jeff loved me and that out of such love babies are born. She was so calm. I relaxed and figured she would take care of everything. But no. The next day she said she'd support me in any decision I made. But she had no advice. She'd help me find an adoption agency or an abortion. She'd drive me to the Florence Crittenton home for unwed mothers or buy a new silk mother-of-the-bride dress for my wedding. She'd let me live with her and Dad and be a single mother, but she wouldn't take care of my baby for me. And she insisted on this: I had to tell Jeff. The baby was half his. I promised her I would, but I couldn't. I was afraid it would spoil things, and I couldn't stand that.

Three months passed and Jeff and I kept driving down country roads and I kept pretending to be carefree. By then it was too cold to lie in the cornfield, but sometimes we'd bring blankets and lie there anyway. We'd point out constellations and tell stories. Jeff liked to point to the east and tell me about Andromeda, who, in Greek legend, was the daughter of an Ethiopian king. For some offense, some boast about beauty that her mother had made, Andromeda was chosen to be sacrificed to the gods. She was chained, naked except for some jewels, to a rock at the edge of the sea. Jeff told me about Andromeda's rescue by Perseus, how Perseus beheaded a sea monster to free her. He told me how that was nothing compared to what he would do for me. I'd stare at the stars, trying to see the configuration in the shape of a much-beloved woman, and believe him. I'd imagine him slaying some monster for me, protecting me, freeing me, loving me forever.

We'd talk about constellations or we'd talk about our pasts or we'd talk about our future together. We didn't know when we'd get married but we knew that we would. We'd talk about which tall tower of apartments we wanted to start our life out in and how we'd decorate our kitchen. We'd talk about names for our babies—Laraine, Melanie, Sabrina. The first would be a boy, he'd be named Jeff. I showed him the bits of leftover yarn my grandmother had given me. I showed him the pattern in her knitting book for a many-colored baby blanket. We'd plan our wedding. Anne-Marie and Sally would be bridesmaids in fuchsia dresses. The best man and ushers would wear cummerbunds to match.

And then one night he found my pants unbuttoned and made a joke about too many french fries. That was the night I told him I was pregnant. I was surprised at his reaction. After I blurted out the truth of it, he grew quiet. This was unlike him. We had always talked.

Afterward, he was silent for days, pretending he hadn't heard me. And then he told me this: He couldn't face it; he'd enlisted in the army. His father had signed for him; he'd leave for boot camp on his eighteenth birthday, only a few months away. He wouldn't even wait for graduation. "No," I screamed, "What about my yarn? What about our wrought-iron kitchen table with matching chairs? What about the map of the stars that would hang in our baby's room? What about me, your beloved, the one you'd kill sea monsters for? What about the Magnavox stereo in our living room where we'd play Temptations albums and Martha and the Vandellas and the Supremes?" I begged him and beat on his chest with my fists but he was steel. He didn't even say he was sorry. Or ask me what I was going to do.

"There's a war going on. My country needs me," was his answer. He turned into a stranger. He was no longer the boy who sang into the wind. Suddenly he was all involved in the Vietnam War and stopping communism. It was a subject that had never come up, all those nights in the cornfield and in the car. All that talking we did, that incessant talking, and he'd never mentioned the war or patriotism or serving anybody but me.

For a week I grieved. For some reason I spent most of that week with Jeff's mother, not with mine. We'd sit on her couch drinking Cokes and eating potato chips and she'd promise me he'd come to his senses and "do right by you, honey." And if he didn't, well, then, "God would punish him." He was acting more and more like his dad, she said, stubborn and selfish. I didn't know if Jeff was more afraid of me or of his mother but he spent the rest of the time, before he went in the army, at his dad's efficiency apartment, a sordid little place full of overstuffed used furniture. It didn't even have a radio. Losing Jeff like this was a heartbreaker for his mother. She didn't get to be with her baby before he went off to war.

I wanted to die that week but then something happened. I started to feel calm and I gave Jeff up in my mind, his music, his pain, his Greek legends. I didn't throw his picture away but I took it off my dresser and put it in a drawer, under my scarves. I ceremoniously laid all his gifts—the opal ring, the cameo brooch, the gardenia corsage from his junior prom—in a box covered with quilted ivory satin and stored it high on a closet shelf.

By then, by the time I was free to think about my baby, it was too late for an abortion, so at least I didn't have to picture what that would entail. That's what my mother said anyway. Perhaps that was her way of expressing the opinion she claimed to refuse to express. Another refusal to pose as the authority in my life. Another chance for me to take responsibility for myself. And I was relieved that I could check off another option, to shorten my list of choices, a list I didn't want to face.

But I did. I faced the list. I decided to give the baby up. I decided it one morning after I'd had a dream about being a mother. My brown hair was bleached blond and stringy and heavy black eyeliner was on my eyelids. Me and the baby lived in a small efficiency full of used, overstuffed furniture with no radio. In the dream I was using a knife as a microphone and doing an imitation of Diana Ross singing "Baby Love, My Baby Love." My hips were swiveling and I felt real cool. My baby started to struggle. I had laid him facedown in a big chair and he started to sputter. The blanket under him had gotten all wadded up around his face and he couldn't get his breath. I knew he might die and I planned to get him, but I wanted to finish my song first. I woke up before either the rescue or the death, but I took the dream as a sign that I wasn't ready.

I stayed in school until my stomach got ridiculous. Then I made an appointment with Sister John Gabriel, the principal. I told her that my family was going to be moving because my father had been transferred. She put her hand on mine and her eyes went soft and understanding and she said she knew the truth of the matter, she had eyes to see and she was sorry. She said she knew this was a painful time for me. I hadn't expected her to believe me, but I had expected her to be cold and cruel. Her kindness took me by surprise and tears washed down my face. She took me in her arms and held my head against the side of hers, and I felt how stiff her starched white cap was under her veil. I cried and cried and she just held me. When I was done, I thanked her. I said I hoped my tears hadn't wilted her habit. She offered me a bar of the World's Finest Chocolate, with almonds, which we sold every year as a fund-raiser.

That was my last day at school. And it was the day I told Sally and Anne-Marie the whole truth. The story I had made up, and that they had believed, was that Jeff and I had broken up because I'd seen a cheerleader from the public school riding in his Spitfire. I had explained that the loss of him made me feel so empty inside that I was filling up with food—hot-fudge ice cream cake, onion rings, Milky Ways, cheeseburgers, whole jars of olives. I couldn't stop eating. They'd given me their pity and their understanding. Both confessed that grief made them overeat too. They were just lucky they hadn't blown up like I had. They were both on the basketball team. I was the sedentary one. We'd talked about it quite a lot. Almost every night on the phone I'd produced a litany of the food I'd consumed that day. They had tried to help: "When you get the urge to eat, drink three glasses of water to give you the sense of fullness," "Always have peeled carrot sticks on hand." They had been into my story.

The truth floored them. Anne-Marie kept covering her face with her hands and saying she couldn't believe it. Sally called Jeff a shit-head over and over. Neither of them had known a pregnant person before, so they had lots of questions. Sally wondered if they should get everyone in our class to sign a petition begging Sister John Gabriel to let me stay in school.

"No," I said. "Just don't forget about me. Without Jeff, without school, I'll really have nothing to do. I'll just be home watching game shows and soaps," I said, "and reading Victoria Holt and Mary Stewart."

But that's not what happened. Our television broke and my mother said we couldn't afford to have it fixed. Even then I knew that was a lie, but I accepted it. I didn't like TV that much anyway. She probably broke it herself, got a screwdriver and took the back off, unscrewed a tube or unhooked a small wire. "Well, no use sitting around here," she said. I'd feel better if I exercised, she said—a radical notion for those days I realize now, but I obeyed her. Every day but Sunday we went swimming at the YWCA pool. I'd move slowly through the cool blue water and imagine that my baby was doing the same thing, moving slowly in the water in my womb, waving his tiny arms, kicking his tiny legs, holding his tiny eyes closed tight. My little swimmer.

We didn't have *in utero* photographs back then, but there were sketches. I checked out a book from the library called *Expectant Motherhood* and learned the words for all my parts, words I'd had introduced to me in sophomore biology but that had seemed to belong only to married women: *fallopian tube, cervix, vaginal canal, uterine lining.* I learned that my bones were going to loosen up, I'd be split, sort of like an earthquake, when it was time for my baby to be born.

Our library didn't have books on how to put your baby up for adoption. I don't remember where we got the phone number that led me to Mrs. Quinn, who told me all about a Catholic couple one state away. She didn't say which way. The man was a member of the Knights of Columbus and the woman was active in the sodality. I bet the number came from Sister John Gabriel. The man was a lawyer and the woman a homemaker who loved to bake and do needlepoint. They'd been married for seven years and God still hadn't given them a child. I thought they sounded OK. I thought about it for a few days, and then I called Mrs. Quinn and told her they could have my baby. I filled out forms.

I got down my bag of yarn and asked my grandmother for the knitting lessons she had promised me. Knit one, purl one. It was soothing to sit in the wing chair in my mother's sewing room and knit. I thought the least I could do for my baby was to give him a many-colored blanket for a birthday present, a going-away present.

My mother's sewing machine was across the room from me and as I knit, she sewed, humming away, making me maternity clothes. My mother made a ridiculous number of dresses for a person who hardly ever went anywhere except the library and the YWCA. But she kept buying great swaths of flowered material and designing me these tents. She didn't want me to get depressed.

My father brought me something every day, just something from the newsstand by his bus stop: a box of lemon drops, a bag of salted peanuts, a strawberry twirler, a *Time* magazine. He'd ask me how I was feeling and smile kindly, but he never mentioned the baby directly. He taught me how to play backgammon and let me help him build a birdhouse down in the basement, at his workbench.

Sister John Gabriel had implored me to keep up with my school-work, "to keep your mind alive." I had planned to do a little algebra every day, a little chemistry, some French, religion, and English, but I got lazy. I remember I read some French plays, one by Corneille and one by Racine and one by Molière. I read each one out loud, alone in my room. The rhythm of their verses put me in the same mood as swimming did. It was soothing, like a lullaby. For some reason it made me feel close to my baby.

My English class the semester I dropped out was British Literature. The only entire novel we were assigned was *David Copperfield*. I read that alone too, in my room. My class hadn't gotten to it before I left. When I first began novels in those days I always had a dictionary and a notebook at my side. Once I got hooked I never bothered to look up a word, but for the first thirty pages or so I was alert for words whose meanings I was unsure of. *Caul* appears on page one of *David Copperfield*, and that was my first entry in my new vocabulary notebook.

So when my baby was born in a caul, I wasn't shocked or appalled. When the doctor pulled away the veil, the membrane, and I could see him more clearly, he didn't look much like the graceful swimmer I had pictured during my pregnancy. He was wrinkled and red faced and greasy.

The next day my mother made me visit him. She walked me down the hall to the nursery and made me look at him through the glass. His eyes were closed, his lips parted in a smile. My mother motioned for the nurse to meet her at the nursery door. The nurse wasn't happy with what my mother said, I could see, but she complied. She handed her a gown and a mask which my mother then handed to me. I put them on. Then she led me into the nursery and told me to sit in the rocking chair. The nurse was mad. She told my mother she was cruel, the baby was being adopted out, what was she trying to do, punish her daughter for getting pregnant in the first place? My mother didn't seem to hear her, she just took the baby from the nurse and gave him to me. She unwrapped his blanket and told me to feel his skin, his hair, and to be sure I was ready to give him up. "Kiss him on the forehead when you're ready to say good-bye," she said.

I put my finger on his arm and moved it up and down. A petal. I touched his black hair and studied his toes. I laid my hand on his stomach and closed my eyes. I tried to conjure up the girl in the efficiency pretending to be Diana Ross. I even hummed her song, "Baby Love, My Baby Love," but I never saw the girl with the heavy black eyeliner and bleached stringy hair. She just wouldn't appear, even though I'd written about her vividly in my journal.

I kissed him on the forehead, but I didn't say good-bye. I held him for most of that day and stared and stared at his face. I called Mrs. Quinn the next day and told her the deal was off. My mother got my old bassinet out of the crawl space and put it next to my bed at home, and she went to a department store and bought him kimonos and diapers and rubber pants.

A few days after we got home I called Jeff's mother and told her my news. She was shocked. I had been so firm in my resolve to give the baby up, she wasn't at all prepared to deal with having a grandbaby. But she was kind and told me she was sure I'd done the right thing, and the next day she came over to visit. She brought a blue sweater-and-bootie set for David (I had decided against naming him Jeff), and she brought a nightgown for me. She brought along Jeff's last letter, full of the rigors of boot camp, and a photograph of Jeff I barely recognized; his head was almost shaved. That day, for the first time in three years, I felt no love for him. When he looked like a soldier, he was a stranger to me.

But the love came back in a few months. I even put his picture back up on my dresser for David to look at. And I kept imagining that he'd come to his senses, that a grenade would explode in front of him in the jungle outside of Da Nang and knock him to his senses, and he'd come home and marry me and move us to our favorite tower of apartments. On Sundays the three of us would picnic in the cornfield.

He did come home before his tour of duty was completed. He was wounded by "friendly fire"—a buddy's gun had gone off accidentally and the bullet had hit Jeff in the leg. His mother called me in secret to tell me he was home. She had written him everything. She was trying to persuade him to at least visit me. He didn't have the courage, it seemed.

David was walking by then. I polished his white high-top shoes, dressed him in a cute sailor outfit, and took him over to meet his father. I had my figure back by then, and my hair was still long. I thought the two of us would be irresistible, sort of. My mother said later that maybe I should have left David with her, if I had really wanted Jeff back.

I don't know if I really wanted Jeff back that day. As I climbed the steps to his mother's door with David on my hip, I saw through the picture window that he was there, sitting at the kitchen table with his mother. He looked anguished. His chin was in his hands. His eyes were closed. His hair was still short. I guessed that they were talking about me.

He didn't kiss me, but he was real nice to me. He told me he was sorry and he even wept a little. He kept staring at David, looking for himself I guess, and trying to make contact with him. But David had found the cupboards with the pots and pans and was much more interested in making a racket than in making a relationship with his long-lost father.

So Jeff wasn't the man of steel he had made himself be when he'd said good-bye to me all those months before. But he wasn't the same as he'd been in the cornfield, either. I could see it on his face—faraway eyes, set teeth, a line beginning between his eyebrows. I guess war changes a person, the way having a baby does. So by the time I said good-bye, by the time I threw my arms around his neck and told him I'd always love him, and told him that having his baby was the best thing in my life, I knew that it was over. I knew there'd never be a wedding with Anne-Marie and Sally in fuchsia.

And having his baby is still the best thing I ever did, nineteen years later. I tell my mother that, and I ask her if she had known it would be, if that's why she insisted I hold and touch his newborn self. But she swears not, she shakes her head adamantly, and says no, she thought that giving him up was the right thing to do. She thought I should have my own life. She didn't want me to be tied down at sixteen, tied down by love and obligations.

My mother is old now, but there are hardly any lines in her face. Her hair is a bright white. She braids it and winds it into a bun at the back of her neck. Her skin always looks tan with her hair so white. Her eyes are a clear blue, like the water in a swimming pool. We sometimes go together now to that YWCA pool where I first pictured David inside me. We do laps side by side, slowly. It seems more meditation than swim sometimes. It seems like a holy place, the swimming pool, like a cornfield, like a church, like a room where a baby is born.

Morning News

Maggi Ann Grace

I hold the paper
sliced in early light,
read past the trial of a father
who powdered
his toddler's disposables with Drano
to inside pages
where an infant was found
locked inside a pickup truck
sucking a beer-filled bottle
while the teen mom window-shopped.
I flip to the back page
where the eight month old found
in an unheated Chicago apartment
won't need amputation after all,
only treatment for frost
and rodent bites.

My coffee is glue
sliding down my throat
and I must dress to pass
parades of mothers,
robeless judges
who tow chapped kids,
balance signs that talk of rights,

not of adolescents
not of men and women
who make mistakes
but rights of the results:
unborns who may be dropped
like bread crumbs on church steps,
in toilet bowls or scalding baths.

Getting Ready

Catherine Boyd

The temperature, as it often does on muggy, overcast days, continued to rise as the afternoon rolled toward evening. About halfway between the big white house and the end of the vineyard, Margo bent over, fitting one shiny irrigation pipe into another. She wore a beige T-shirt, spackled with mud, a navy-blue one-piece bathing suit underneath. Her skin was tanned dark; the working muscles were wet and they flashed in the gray light.

She walked to the end of a twenty-foot pipe, resting in a muddy ditch between two rows of tiny grapes. She inserted the pipe into the next one, gave it a hard twist followed by a test pull. She sloshed along the ditch to the unattached end, where another pipe waited. Instinctively, she felt someone coming. She looked across the field of green leaves and saw Eric walking her way.

He waved and smiled. "Hello there!" he yelled, waving a second time.

"Hello," she called back. "I was hoping you'd find me." Starting at her bare feet, she traced the warm mud to her hips and waist. She laughed nervously—not because he was seeing her like this—but because of what she planned on telling him.

When Eric reached Margo, he took her in his arms and gave her a long kiss. "I missed you," he said.

She wrapped her hands around the back of his neck, moved with his hug, and stared at the playground of her childhood, a one-acre pond. These last three weeks, awake every night, sweating so much the sheet had become pasted to her breasts, Margo would throw a towel around herself, sneak out of the house, and walk along the grape rows to the pond. She would swim freestyle to the other side, take handfuls of silty black mud and rub it on her stomach, trying to decide what to do.

She patted his sides and stepped back. "Let's go to the pond. It seems cooler there." She reached for his hand, and they walked to the wooden diving dock.

"Where's your mom?" Eric asked. "I didn't see her car."

Margo let go of his hand and sat. Her feet dangled in the water. "She went to the store. Whenever you come, it's like suddenly we have to eat big meals."

He kicked off his shoes and socks, and sat next to her, legs in the water. He took a deep breath. "You sure it's OK for you to be doing work like this? In your condition?"

Her head dropped back and she watched a turkey vulture glide a slow, wide circle. "I feel strong as a horse." She turned to him, threw out her right arm and flexed the bicep. "What do you think?"

His foot touched hers. "I think we should be talking about it. Once your mom gets back it will be nothing but social stuff."

Margo pulled off her T-shirt and shook out her hair. She dropped into the water.

His feet kicked involuntarily. He said, "I feel like something's wrong."

She grabbed his ankles, holding them still. "There is something I've got to tell you."

He leaned forward and touched the tops of her shoulders. "Before you say anything, I want you to know there's no hurry. I'm not going to try to push you either way."

Standing in the oozing silt, she looked across the vineyard at the slow up-and-down vibrations of the heat waves. She held on to him and quietly spoke: "I went to town last week, and I had one."

He was sweating heavily. He swallowed hard, swallowed again. "You had one? What the hell does that mean?"

"I had it last Friday. At a clinic in Stockton. Don't worry, I used a fake name."

Eric looked blankly at the pond. "Jesus, Margo, I just talked to you on the phone *yesterday*."

"It's not the kind of thing you tell someone over the telephone."

"But I would have gotten a day off work and met you there. I would have gone *in* with you." He rubbed his forehead. Almost to himself, he said, "Oh, I get it. You needed to do it alone."

Margo held her mouth tight, to keep from trembling. She turned around so she wouldn't have to look at him.

Eric took off his shirt and joined her in the pond. They swam across to where a four-inch pipe delivered pumped well water. They took turns pressing their bodies against the cold current. Margo took care to not let the powerful flow hit her low on the belly.

Without speaking, she headed back. Eric followed. They climbed onto the dock and, faces down, stretched out on the baking planks. They dried quickly in the sun.

"Did you ever think about what it would look like? If it would be a boy or a girl?" Margo asked.

"A little, sometimes. But not as much as I thought it could foul things up for us—in the long run. You know what I mean," he said.

"It seems to me a baby would be pretty innocent as far as messing up our lives goes."

Eric turned and wrapped his arms around her. He kissed the back of her neck. "I wish you would have called me." He hugged her tightly from behind.

Margo reached over the side of the dock and trailed a hand through the tepid water. She wanted so badly to hear him say he had wanted the baby, but that it just wasn't practical, or realistic, or smart. She wanted to hear him say that part of him wished she could have had it. She wished to God he would tell her he felt the same way she did.

"Listen to me," he said. "You did the right thing. The *best* thing." He stayed nuzzled against her. "Margo, please, talk to me. Tell me what you're thinking."

She turned and looked at him. "I think it's different for women."

"It must be. It can't be easy to give up a piece of yourself."

Her thoughts sped out in all directions, stretching the already worn fabric of her mind. She started to cry—and said, "I'll be all right. I'll be fine."

"Of course you'll be all right. It's just going to take time. There's always a certain shock afterwards with something like this."

But she had lied to him. She hadn't gone to Stockton. She had lied to him because ever since they had found out she was pregnant he had acted more like a close friend than a father. He'd given her advice, and little else. She needed him to take a stand. She needed to know what he really felt before she went ahead with her decision. "It's funny it bothers me so much." She choked on her choppy breathing, started again. "It's not like I'm against abortions, not at all. It's just that I'm not for them. No matter how many times you turn it over in your head, it's bad either way."

Eric ran his hand down her spine. "It was the only thing you could do, Margo. I feel lousy about it too."

Although she had known all along that she would make the trip to the clinic in Stockton, and use a fake name, she hadn't been able to get herself to feel ready. Now she was close to ready.

"C'mon, let's go inside and take a shower," Margo said. They helped each other up from the dock. "My mom's going to be back pretty soon and I want to help her with dinner."

Spiderplant

Terri L. Jewell

i watch you
push out earth
thick yellow anchors
shove unwilling babies
into air
along slim tendrils
bearing fruit
and flower
i choose a
golden barrenness
while full of seed
plant a prudent crop
libations to the south
dream my own acreage
of sacred ground

Life Support

Dorothy Howe Brooks

It has been only three weeks since she first came to this room, this intensive-care neonatal unit, yet it seems to Cynthia that she has had no life outside, no life before. The clock on the wall of the newborn nursery, visible through the glass partition beside her, is her only contact with the passing time. The fluorescent daylight begins at 6:00 A.M., ends at 9:00 P.M. John brings her a newspaper each day when he stops in for his early morning visit, and this way she keeps track of the days. If it weren't for John she would have to chalk a primitive mark on the pure white wall behind her each time the lights went on.

Beside the chair where she now sits, there is a cot. Nearby, a small, black-and-white television, a writing table where she eats, and a bookcase with well-read copies of *McCall's, Science Today, Parent*. Directly in front of her, not quite close enough to touch, is the machine, the large steel structure with the glass womb where her baby, Michael, lives. He wears patches to preserve his eyesight, and a miniature diaper. Wires and tubes taped carefully onto his tiny body connect him to receptor points in the machine. Above the glass housing are dials, switches, and a glowing console with regular graphic patterns appearing and disappearing to measure and regulate his breathing, his heartbeat, his nourishment. Just above his diaper, the oversized stub of an umbilical cord, almost healed, shows Cynthia how recently her own body gave him life support.

It is seven-thirty. John has just left for work. Cynthia stretches, stiff from another night on the hard cot. John wants her home, says he needs her, but she can't leave. Her body is mending. The swelling in her stomach is gradually returning to normal, her breasts, large with anticipation of the child to nurse, have lost their milk. She places her hands over her empty womb as she often held them during the past eight months when she could feel the new life quicken beneath them, and looks to the infant. She has never held him.

She gets up and goes to the glass incubator. She reaches her hands through the openings designed to ensure that even these sick babies feel their mother's touch, and strokes his forehead. He never responds. The doctors say he may already have been deprived too long of oxygen, may never respond. They do know that without this machine he would be dead. Cynthia thinks maybe he is already dead, maybe he died, alone, in a moment that she cannot now recapture.

On the table is the form John brought her this morning. It is a consent form for surgery. The tests they have been doing for the past three weeks have finally yielded a tentative answer. His heart is defective. His only hope is surgery, delicate microsurgery on his heart. His chances are not good. She and John must consent. They hold him in the balance. Her choice this morning is to consent or watch him in this glass bubble forever.

Cynthia feels there must be other choices. She wants to unplug the machine, snatch her baby back, and cradle him. She longs to hold him to her barren breast and rock him, to sing to him all the lullabies that she practiced when he was safe inside of her. But there is no plug, no master attachment she can safely sever to steal back her child. And there are nurses around the clock looking in who would save him from her.

In quiet moments Cynthia thinks back to the night in the delivery room when her nightmare began. It seemed a normal birth. The black hair of the head crowned. John squeezed her hand in his excitement. One more push and the infant emerged, covered in white mucous and bits of blood. But he wouldn't cry, couldn't breathe. The doctors whisked him away. A nurse gave her a sedative, asked John to leave. When she awoke in the recovery room, John told her their baby was alive but only barely. She lifted up in the bed and reached for John, held him close and tight, and they cried together.

Though she can see the well babies in the next room, she can hardly imagine that only three weeks ago they expected, even assumed, they would have such a child. A child peacefully sleeping, breathing on his own without the aid of the steel machine. It is difficult even to imagine such a child, though she sees them every day. Looking at Michael, it seems impossible that such a tiny thing could exist on its own, disconnected, apart from any life support, just as it seems impossible to suppose that she and John had a life before this room.

She picks up the consent form and reads it again. "Little or no anesthesia..." A stumbling block. The doctors explained that his chances were so slim they couldn't risk putting him to sleep. They would use some local anesthetics to reduce the pain, but they couldn't know what he might feel. They told her the latest research indicates newborns feel very little pain. Very little pain. She repeats the words to herself as she walks again to the tiny body. She reaches her hands in again to stroke him. Very little pain. Who is to measure the pain?

This morning, John hugged her and said she must sign. He said he knew how difficult it was for her, it was just as difficult for him, but she must sign. It was their only hope, Michael's only hope. We have to do what's best for Michael, he'd said. She has been a mother only three weeks yet her child is depending on her to know what is right, to do what is best.

Her instincts are false. Her instincts tell her to grab him, to hold him, and that would kill him. Her reason must prevail. Medical science must prevail. She looks up at the dials, the green monitor charting its regular course. Life in the steady, rhythmic patterns. She looks at her child and it feels like death, not life, the machine is preserving. A death machine, postponing death, altering it, shaping it.

She sees the form on the table waiting for her, demanding her attention. She knows she will sign. But she will sign the way she has done everything these past three weeks, as if she was in a fog, groping. She wishes she could sign with courage, with conviction, with hope.

As she lies back in the chair and rests her head on a soft pillow, she has a dream. It is not quite a dream for she is not quite asleep. It is a scene that comes to her in those suspended moments between waking and sleep. It is this: She is in labor again. The head crowns and the infant emerges, covered in white mucous tinged with blood. His eyes are shut against the light, but his breathing comes, shallow but steady.

She opens her nightgown and John takes the infant and places him directly on her breasts. Skin touches skin. The umbilical cord extends but is not yet cut. She strokes the tiny head, the cap of black hair, holds the tiny body close and tight against her. The limp form, so newly come from the womb, molds itself to her, to her large breasts, her rounded belly. The tiny head burrows into her, searching instinctively for the nipple. She finds it and brings it to his lips and he sucks, though there is no milk yet to nourish him. Then his movements stop, his breathing becomes faint, his chest no longer pulses in its regular rhythm. He looks as if he is asleep but Cynthia knows he is not, knows he is gone. She is calm. She doesn't cry out or call for help because in the dream— and this is how she knows, finally, that it is a dream—she is certain of what he needs.

Art As Life

Ann Menebroker

It's about stillness,
a feeling for the primitive spirit,
displaced structure,
and someone listening, lying
in her single bed
by a window
shadow and light
making canvas figures
upon the walls,
breathing slowly,
taking it all in
as if she were, for this moment,
the only person on earth
who finally hears
what is being missed,
who finally sees
what has been overlooked,
who touches herself
slowly, to feel who she is
through flesh, this minimal
product
of skeletal remains,
who then turns sideways
from the view,
closing her eyes, but
retaining the image, sleeps
with a smile on her lips.

Photo by Lori Burkhalter-Lackey

Résumé

Dori Appel

When her life seemed
too demanding, my mother often
claimed it was her sole ambition
to stand in some monotonous
factory line, watching cans
of beans roll by. She wouldn't
mind the pay because
her simple job would be to drop
a piece of pork
on top of each. On better days
she craved a business
of her own, some classy place
with her name on the awning that
she ruled in a good gray suit.

Now the direction of her gaze
has changed. She focuses on what
she hasn't been—a faster reader,
better shopper, thin. As she recites
her litany of disappointment,
I see her in that scheme she once
imagined: A conveyer belt
is humming, and a thousand cans are
floating by like objects in a dream.
Beneath the cool fluorescent lights
my mother lifts her hand—a girl
with a paycheck coming,
and nothing but
this moment on her mind.

Mother Land

Linda Wasmer Smith

I knew that place like the freckles I tried to bleach
With lemon juice across my nose. I knew
The geometric grace of fields that reach
Beyond the point where green caresses blue.
I knew the fertile Mississippi muck
That sprouts soybeans and weeds that spread like fire
Through hay. Sometimes I believed I might be stuck
Forever, deep in that tenacious mire.
I never really came to know that place,
I never knew the life-force in my blood
That slows all movement to the seasons' pace.
I pulled myself free like a shoe from the mud
And left. Now from books, my children understand
The concept Farm. They'll never know the land.

A Woman's Choice

Jacklyn W. Potter

1.

The black coat. *It's the key to fashion.*
She wants it. The one with the collar
that won't quit, the midcalf, pure wool
black coat—the limit, the essence,
half-price, the black coat. She wants it.

She tries it: the perfect coat.
She is particular, precise,
she is the woman in the black coat.
See her seduce the bay!
See her lie in iridescent foam!
Soft wool rides the waves.

Now she gives it
back to the rack.

2.

As she watches the boats
that go for clams and scallops,
the wind slaps her,
the wind that wears kid gloves.
She has consumed
many heads of lettuce,
she has picked
at many bones of fish.

Each day she repeats
a thousand motions,
she gathers her heart and body
at last, home, to the place
of her solitary choosing.
The sea gulls wing before her window screen.
She wears her skin alone to bed.

Máire, Who Feeds the Wild Cat?

Pat Schneider

For Máire O'Donohoe

Behind the convent a wild
cat is ill. She sleeps
in a fine mist of rain
on the warm hood
of a cooling automobile.
She's sick, poor thing,
you say. You say
she's too sick to run away.

And you are cloistered here
uneasy now in all
the old, familiar habits,
awkward in the raw world,
its own severe conventions,
language of fashion,
innuendos. Rules.

From the window of the guesthouse
I study the convent walls,
the remote third floor
where no one may go but
nuns of your particular order.
The wall is fortress high
and fortress thick. Inside,

the sisters smile, repeating
and repeating one another's names:
Rosario, Saint Ambrose, Immaculate.

Outside, where a mist of rain
has chilled the bone of this day,
a wild cat watches,
too sick to run away.

Photo by Lori Burkhalter-Lackey

Imaginary Bonds

Bonnie Michael

Like rings around Saturn
the furies of her life encircle her.
Not knowing she is the planet,
she gives them power.

Her prison sky looms endlessly.
Her other lives were long ago;
she cannot seem to remember them,
cannot seem to find their moons.

When the time is right, she will know
the galaxy is more than Saturn—
she is not held by imaginary bonds
nor blinded by falling stars.

The Scorpion Wore Pink Shoes

Janice Levy

"*Despiértate,* wake up, Soledad!" Clara hissed.

Soledad groaned and rubbed her eyes.

"Come on, *ya se hace tarde,* it's getting late, and we have a lot to do."

Squinting through one eye, Soledad saw that Clara was already wearing her gray dress and white apron, the name Harrington Hotel stitched over its top pocket. Crescents of sweat darkened the cotton uniform under her arms. Soledad stretched slowly, her aching legs sticking up under the white sheet of her cot. She coughed up the phlegm that stuck in her throat like lumps of glue. She felt like a leftover meal.

As Clara pushed her cleaning cart filled with disinfectants, toilet scrub brushes, and plastic bags out of the basement, she gestured with her nose at Soledad to hurry. The housekeeping staff lived in the basement of the Harrington Hotel in New Hampshire, with sheets hung across the ceiling to separate the cots. Soledad's bed was closest to the row of washing machines. She stared at the clothes spinning around and wondered how it would feel to be sucked up and tossed about until you became just a blur of color.

She threw off her blanket and walked stiffly to one of the dryers to take out some pillowcases and sheets. She rested her head on top of a whirring machine and imagined herself slow dancing, her body pressed against the warm chest of a handsome man. The deep, soothing noise of the machine reminded her of Geraldo's humming in the shower, while she lingered in bed and inhaled his scent from the sheets. But that was a long time ago, when she had been almost as young as her daughter, Gabriela, was now, and there was still a reason to linger.

When Clara's friend, Mr. Jones, came to Costa Rica looking for women to bring back to the States with him, Soledad left her job at the factory where her boss stood with a watch to make sure she scaled and gutted fifteen fish an hour. She asked her mother to take care of Gabriela. "You'll see, *Mamá*, I'll send you money so the doctors can take the veins out of your legs and Gabriela can go to the *universidad* to study."

She told her daughter she would come back in a year. *"Te prometo, I promise."* Gabriela had stared at her with lizard eyes. Mr. Jones wore a toupee that looked like a dead pigeon and his cheeks were the color of an emery board. He got Soledad a tourist visa and a social security card that changed her into "Maria Rivera," a Puerto Rican from New York. When she started working in the hotel, she sometimes leaned against the door of a room before knocking and strained to make sense of the words that shot out in English as fast as gunfire. But after six months, she could say little more than, "Good morning," "Sorry," and "Room clean?"

Clara learned English because she cleaned Mr. Jones's house on her day off. Soledad saw her friend and Mr. Jones coming out of the service elevator together early one morning; Clara's face had been flushed and her hair messed up. Clara said you could make fifty dollars in four hours, but you had to be smart.

Every Sunday night, Soledad made a three-minute phone call to Costa Rica, covering one ear with her hand to block out the noise from the hallway. While waiting their turns on the long line that snaked down the hall, the maids passed around letters and pictures. Soledad's mother had sent her a picture of Gabriela, standing with Gabriela's father, Geraldo, in front of a neighbor's house. Gabriela was, at fourteen, as tall as Soledad, and already wore her mother's shoes and clothes. In the photograph, she stood slumped forward, her fists rolled up under her chin, her head tilted away from her father. Geraldo had one hand on her shoulder. Soledad couldn't make out her daughter's face clearly, but she knew how her daughter was feeling. Gabriela didn't like to be touched. By anyone. Ever.

Geraldo faced the camera, mustachioed and heavy-lidded, with his hips jutting forward. Soledad remembered how just touching his thigh lightly with her fingertips used to make her legs turn to jelly. In the six months Soledad had been in the United States, she had received one letter from Geraldo, the handwriting smeared and running up and down the page like crawling worms. Soledad heard he had remarried. She wondered if he hit his new wife in the face after yelling at her.

On the telephone, Gabriela spoke excitedly about her upcoming *quinceañera*. In another month she would be fifteen years old. Gabriela thanked Soledad for sending the money to buy fabric so *Abuelita* Rosa could make the dress for her big party. But now the problem was finding a pair of matching shoes.

"I've looked everywhere, in all the stores, and I can't find anything I like. They have to be perfect."

Soledad could picture her sullen daughter pacing up and down and frowning.

"I want shoes that a princess would wear: princess slippers, with high, high heels. And pink. They've got to be pink."

When Soledad asked if she had chosen an escort for her party, she heard Gabriela take a deep breath, and she knew her daughter was tapping her foot up and down.

"Yes, *Mami.* I asked Juan, but don't worry because we're not *novios;* he's just my friend. But, so anyway, about the shoes, you won't forget to send the money for them, OK?"

Soledad wiped her eyes when her daughter used up the last moments of the phone call with kisses.

Soledad knocked on the door of the first room she had to clean. She opened the door with her key and pushed her cleaning cart into the center of the room. Holding her breath, she emptied the overflowing ashtrays. She put clean glasses with paper tops on the dresser, replaced the stationery in the drawers, and filled a little wicker basket in the bathroom with bottles of shampoo and conditioner. As Soledad filled a vase with water and added a red carnation, she thought of her mother's house, where she had returned after Geraldo had left her lying on the kitchen floor. The house was small, and the color of tarnished silver. The roof was wooden; the balcony a slab of colored stones. On the front porch steps, Soledad had placed red flowers in brightly painted tin cans. She painted the cans herself, with images of fuchsia-feathered roosters and scampering little black pigs, all of the things she saw while she sat on the porch and waited for Geraldo to make it all good again.

When he did, it was always the same. He'd bring *Mama* Rosa some flowers, swing Gabriela in the air, and toss his hat across the room for Soledad to catch. Soledad would cook his favorite dishes and wash his clothes. She'd stroke his face and lay her head on his chest. Once, Geraldo stayed for a few weeks and they took a trip to Póas, the volcano, outside the city of Alajuela. As the taxi huffed its way on the winding roads, through the green fields and small farms, Geraldo chewed on her ear and played with her hair. They walked, arms around each other, up the trail to the crater of the volcano. As they walked through the forest of clouds, Soledad matched her breathing to Geraldo's and thought his face looked like *un ángel del cielo.*

Soledad sighed and threw off the sheets and put them in her laundry bag. She remade the bed and put on fresh pillowcases. She hugged a pillow and closed her eyes. Those were the times to remember, she thought. Not the times when Geraldo paced the house and scratched himself like a dog in heat, went out at night and came back stumbling and falling against things. He'd come back later and later, until Soledad knew he was finally gone, because the only sounds in the house when the sun came up were the muffled sobs of Gabriela and the ticking of a clock.

Soledad pushed her cart down the hall to Suite 710, the best accommodations on the floor, with a living room, a fireplace in the bedroom, and a telephone in the bathroom. She picked up the breakfast tray from the floor and put the leftover rolls and packets of orange marmalade in her pocket. Several bottles of perfume, all opened, sat on the bathroom sink, their tops lying nearby. A makeup case floated in the half-filled bathtub, forming lily pads of greasy rainbows on the water's surface. False eyelashes swirled like drowning spiders under the faucet. Soledad shut off the dripping water and walked into the living room. Three fur coats were rolled up on the couch—they looked like drunks holding their stomachs. A purple suede hat with a corkscrew stuck through its brim sat in a bucket of melted ice on the bar's countertop. Soledad looked at the wine stains on the bed sheets and the broken champagne glasses on the hearth. She suddenly felt tired and looked around for a clean place to sit down.

Flung over the back of a chair was a man's tuxedo and a pink gown with a neckline of white feathers. She ran her hand down the front of the dress, over a big orange stain, touching sequins and beads and pearls, some hanging by loose threads. A cigarette had burned a hole over the left shoulder.

As a bead from the gown fell into her hand, Soledad thought of her daughter's *quinceañera* dress. Gabriela wanted a traditional dress, down to the floor, tight on top and full at the bottom, with a skirt shaped like a wedding bell. She mailed a sketch of the dress to Soledad, along with a piece of material, and for weeks, Soledad kept the swatch of pink satin with tiny white rosebuds on it in the pocket of her uniform. When she touched it, she could almost see Padre Vargas, the pastor at the *Iglesia de Cristo*, giving her daughter the blessing at the *quinceañera* mass, just as he had blessed Soledad, sixteen years ago, making the sign of the cross as she knelt in front of him. Soledad remembered her own *quinceañera* and her tall, handsome escort who danced a kind of waltz with her, weaving in and out among the other fourteen girls and their escorts, forming small and then big circles, like the ripples on a pond. She had stood with all the girls on the sidewalk outside the church, giggling when a car drove by and made a great poof that made their full dresses fly up. Soledad fingered the cross around her neck and thought of the *Iglesia de Cristo*, with its hard wood pews and a ceiling so high it made her neck hurt to see its top. The stained glass behind the altar glistened in the sunlight like multicolored dewdrops. Soledad wondered if Padre Vargas still kept a pail hanging outside the side door of the church for the children to deposit their bubble gum in.

Soledad held the pink gown against her body and looked in the mirror. Her tall, dark escort had flirted and danced with all the girls, but he caught her eye with a look, quiet and still, like a gift held just out of reach. In back of the church, against a tree in the woods, he took her hair and tied it under her chin so it framed her face like a bonnet. He held her so close that she could feel his eyelashes on her cheeks.

"*Te necesito,* I need you, Soledad," he had pleaded.

Soledad had let him find his way past the bows and ties of her dress, under the satin slips. His face had looked like a wounded bird, so she had held him and stroked his head until he shivered and stopped.

After they were married, Soledad and Geraldo lived with his parents in Sarchi, northwest of San José, the capital. Geraldo worked with his father building ox carts that the farmers used to carry their coffee beans. *Turistas* liked to watch them work in the open sheds. Soledad painted geometric designs on the ox carts and listened to Geraldo practice his English with the men in baggy shorts and gold watches, men with cameras around their necks. Geraldo told them the wheels he carved made music as they turned.

He winked and smiled at the overdressed ladies in high heels and ropes of jewelry. He took them by the hand and set them down in his handmade, wood rocking chairs. He took off his hat and fanned them, using a mixture of Spanish and English to describe their beauty. Almost always the men bought something, if only to get their wives out of the rocking chairs, because Soledad knew the señoras could sit there forever, giggling and running their fingers through their hair.

Once Geraldo caught a man with a big belly and baseball cap wiping paint off Soledad's cheek with a handkerchief, then opening his wallet and pointing to her. Geraldo had grabbed Soledad by the back of her neck and dragged her behind the shed. He covered her mouth so she wouldn't frighten away the *turistas*. Many hours later, Geraldo pinned her against the bed and squeezed her wrists as if he were stapling her to the sheets. He pushed his weight against her again and again until he had felt the blood rush down her legs and then he fell asleep with his legs across her hips. Soledad rolled out from under him and walked outside to sit in the darkness. She wondered if the man with the big belly and baseball cap was showing his wallet to other women that night or if he made love gently and so quietly that his wife wept. When she counted back, she knew that was the night Gabriela was conceived.

With a heavy sigh, Soledad began wiping the mirrors with glass cleaner. As she pulled down hard on the curtain cord to bring in more light from the high windows overlooking a little terrace, she tripped over a pair of shoes that lay behind the curtain.

The shoes were pink satin with tiny white rosebuds. The toes of the shoes were open except for a transparent lace covering that looked like a bridal veil. The inner side of the shoes curved toward the middle like the waistline of a young girl. Little silver chains of pearls were strung around the heels, which were several inches high. Soledad cradled the shoes in her hands and noted the soles looked clean and a piece of the price tag had not been scraped off one of them.

"Maybe he carried her all night," she said to herself. "Maybe in his arms like a *princesa*." Soledad looked to find the size of the shoes. She slipped them on her feet and smiled. She held out her gray uniform and curtsied to the mirror. Soledad spun around the room, her arms moving like the waves of an ocean. As she arched her neck and pointed her toes, she pretended she was a rich lady, having returned to Costa Rica. She imagined she was making the eight-hour train ride with a lover, from San José to Puerto Limón, to vacation by the Caribbean Sea. They would dangle their hands out the windows and pass through the shoulders of huge mountains, into tangled jungles, along the Reventazón River with its rapids and high rocks. They would see white sand and blue seas and palm trees that looked like feather dusters as they swayed in the wind. Her lover would buy her peanuts and *papas calientes,* hot potatoes, from the small boys who jumped on the trains and sold them down the aisles. The barefooted ladies who wore aprons would call her Doña Soledad and stand before her selling yucca and hot fish. Her lover would snap his fingers in the air and a man would run over with a paper cone filled with bits of ice, berry red with fruit juice. Soledad and her lover would share one and lick their lips, melting the ice in each others' mouths with their tongues. She would put her feet in his lap and he'd take off her pink shoes with the white rosebuds and lightly kiss her ankles, never taking his eyes off her face.

Soledad caught sight of herself in the mirror, her hair messed and swirly. She untied the belt of her uniform and her stomach protruded forward. Soledad shook her head as she took off the shoes. *"Ay, Soledad, que tonta eres,* how silly you are," she said. She thought of her serious, amber-eyed daughter and wondered if Gabriela still believed in the magic of such things.

Soledad heard voices coming from the hall and quickly put the shoes behind the curtain, in the same corner where she had found them. She looked at the clock and realized she would have to work extra fast to finish cleaning all the rooms on the seventh floor. Soledad jumped as a man walked into the room, stumbling as if he had a third leg that kept bumping into the other two. A woman wearing a bathing suit and clumps of jewelry at her ears and throat pushed past him. Soledad thought she looked like a doll whose hair grew when you pressed its stomach, a doll she had once bought for Gabriela. The woman looked at Soledad and scrunched up her eyes, nose, and lips. She shook her fingers in the air as if shooing away pigeons. She threw her purse on the floor, kicked her shoes off, and fell back on the bed. The man said something to Soledad and then repeated it louder. He opened his eyes so wide his eyelashes reached up to his eyebrows. He pointed around the room and spoke louder and louder, his earlobes turning as red as the rising liquid of a thermometer. Soledad bit her lip and said, "Good morning, sorry, clean room?" in one fast breath and quickly pushed her cleaning cart out of the room.

That night, Soledad dreamed of two scorpions mating. The male and female moved back and forth, front legs gripping front legs, mouth parts locked together. The male whipped his tail forward and stung the female again and again, dragging her thrashing body around a dance floor. The female wore pink shoes with white rosebuds. A band played a waltz; then the music switched to mariachi sounds and the female, heavy in her ruffled dress, bit off the male's head and kicked it with the point of her shoe.

Soledad woke up, sticky with sweat. She stood on tiptoe to look out the basement windows. A light snow was falling, the first snowfall Soledad had ever seen. The branches of the trees, stiff under the flakes, made her think of crinoline; the patches of frozen pond reminded her of icing on a cake.

As she watched the sun scratch away the night, Soledad covered her cheeks with her hands and tapped the sides of her head with her fingers. She pushed her tongue hard against the back of her front teeth. Soledad dressed quickly. As she pushed her cleaning cart out into the hall, she saw Mr. Jones walking toward her, waving a piece of paper. Bulky in his dark fur coat and hat, he looked like a circus bear to Soledad.

"Buenos dias, good morning," he said. "Getting an early start today?" He spoke in broken Spanish. "There's been a change in one of your rooms. The people in Suite 710 had some kind of an emergency and they checked out late last night. I think they flew out to Canada. The new guests are checking in early, before noon. So start on the suite first."

Soledad nodded and Mr. Jones reached out and pushed a strand of her hair behind her ear. "I hear you've got a daughter who wants to go to college? If you're looking to make some extra money, let me know. Your friend Clara tells me you're real smart."

Soledad jerked her cleaning cart forward and bumped into a standing ashtray. She could hear Mr. Jones laughing as she reached the service elevator. Soledad took the elevator to the seventh floor. The hall was quiet, except for the sound of a baby crying. She ran to Suite 710. She saw the Do Not Disturb sign lying in a breakfast tray outside the door. Soledad pushed the door open. Wet towels stuck like leeches against the chairs. Orange juice from a pink-rimmed glass dripped onto the pillows. The floor looked like the bottom of a hamster cage, with its piles of ripped-up newspapers and bits of half-eaten food. Soledad quickly made her way across the room to the windows that overlooked the terrace. Biting her knuckles, she drew open the curtains and looked into the corner.

"Soñadora, dreamer," she said, spitting out the words. "What did you expect?"

Soledad straightened her shoulders and roughly tugged at her gray uniform. She thought of Mr. Jones and shivered. She looked at the top of the dresser for a tip and brushed aside some dirty tissues and empty cigarette packs until she found an envelope. Soledad put the three dollars in her pocket and walked toward the door to get her cleaning cart. She threw the empty envelope at the garbage pail, but it landed on the floor. She bent down and stuffed the envelope, hard this time, into the pail. It was then that she felt the blood pound in her ears as she pulled out the pair of shoes—princess slippers, pink with white rose-buds, and high, high heels.

Good Intentions

Doris Vanderlipp Manley

Someday you will tell your children about a woman
who left behind a trail of abandoned projects

husbands never sure of ownership
children never certain of devotion

carvings begun in heat and left unfinished
until discarded in another move

paintings she intended to redo
to catch the true brilliance of the scene

friends she wanted to help in time of trial
but managed only to blow a poem their way

dresses she started making but by the time
she finished them her taste or the weather had changed

cookies burned to a crisp and cakes that fell
when the housewife was submerged by the scholar.

From this conglomeration which makes a life
what will you remember? A woman no more

substantial than a cloud—yet one who caught
the sun.

Sunspots

Barbara Lucas

The late afternoon sun makes islands
across the winter lawn—
spots of time, I call them—
somehow more intense
than the great swaths of summer.
The light enters me, filling dry wells
until I become my own sun.
My fifty years flare to corona
and I walk in a body of gold—
my nuptials to winter.

But I know I can't live on islands.
I must cross their blue borders
into the slashed eye of wind
and ululation of brown leaves.
Whatever I've conceived
must be born into this cold.
Women who choose islands
also choose the sea.

On the Nature of Sin

Sandra Redding

"Have a toke?"

I look at the cigarette my son holds out to me. "Don't think so. Might be a sin."

"You're a hoot, Mama Grace. You know that?"

Some might think my son peculiar for believing in square-shaped planets and polka-dot aliens, but not transgression. "We all have our dark side," he's tried explaining. "But the dark side has nothing whatsoever to do with wrongdoing. It's like right and left, up and down. It takes some of each, both light and dark, to form a person."

John Willis spends most Sundays reading science fiction. I suppose that's where he gets his pagan notions.

He's not the only one confused. Some of those church women have it muddled too, only the exact opposite from John Willis. According to their crazy quilt way of thinking, almost anything a person decides to do, including movie watching and shag dancing, is S-I-N.

Ginny Ledbetter's one of them. Has been for more than twenty-five years. She teaches a Bible study group, I understand, and testifies regularly about wrongdoings here in Spero. Every Sunday morning, she and the rest of the choir dress in maroon robes and sing love songs to Jesus.

With her adoration finished, she prisses about the churchyard, robe still on, plain-faced, not even a smudge of lipstick, spouting off *my* transgressions, as if she really *knows*, to anyone who hasn't already left for home and fried chicken.

"You something, you know that?" When John Willis grins, I gladly forget Ginny Ledbetter and her sanctimonious sisters. Smoke from his funny-smelling cigarette drifts my way. I sneeze.

I know he makes them from papers he keeps in a tin box decorated with silver stars and gray crumbled leaves and seeds he keeps in the bottom kitchen drawer. Most turn out skinny and bent.

He is not the only young man in Spero who smokes these cigarettes, but most keep such business from their mamas. Not John Willis. If he wants to do something, he does it come pestilence or flood. He claims it's my fault. "Guess I take being willful from you," he's often told me.

I can't deny.

John Willis took a shower before I brought the chicken casserole, but his longish hair and beard still haven't dried out. At the moment, he wears bright yellow bathing trunks and green flip-flops. In the summertime it's his usual way of dressing. If he decides to go to the pool, he adds dark glasses, coated purple to protect his eyes from cancer rays, and a shirt covered with orange parrots and palm leaves.

My boy turns up the volume of the puny radio he carries in his pocket. After placing the earphones back over his ears, he begins strumming an invisible guitar. Soon, he's hopping and gyrating about the room, his belly bouncing. When he finishes such shenanigans, he starts in on me again. "Won't hurt nothing," he says. "Why deny yourself a simple pleasure?"

"Pleasure *always* has a price," I remind him before crunching on a cube of ice from my tea glass.

I puzzle on why he's being so insistent. Usually we do not pester one another. John Willis does whatever he fancies and I do whatever I fancy, but today he seems hell-bent on converting me to his way of thinking. Talking on about the merits of those cigarettes, he becomes almost as fanatical as Ginny pandering her negative religion. He speaks of bright colors and powerful smells. His mind, he says, has been sharpened, expanded so that a single thing slows, as if it might go on forever.

I'm almost sixty, I tell him. I can't afford slowdowns.

"Ah-law," he says, finally giving up. He pulls out a chair and sits down at the table with me again. "Certainly enjoyed the casserole, Mama. Certainly did. None better. Not in all of Spero."

"I'll bring macaroni and cheese tomorrow."

"You'll spoil me."

"Already have."

The room we sit in contains a sleeper-sofa that's a putrid shade of green, but John Willis has brightened it up with zebra-striped pillows. On the mosaic cocktail table, rescued from a dumpster, he's placed a robust philodendron that snakes down the side. There's not much else. Only the table we sit at and a park bench, paint peeling, knife-carved names still visible, a stop sign, and a bigger than life-size poster of some bare-chested female. I don't know who.

My boy, I suppose, does the best he can.

Because he's enrolled in refrigeration courses at the technical college, he now works only three nights a week at the Handy Pantry, so he hasn't much money for furniture, or food. What little's left after rent, he probably wastes on music tapes and smoking supplies.

When John Willis smiles, his eyes close, forming slits that resemble new moons. He gets that from my side, and the way the skin between his eyebrows scrunches, forming two lines when he frowns. His lankiness comes from me, too, and ears that stick too close to his head. Also the small sliver of birthmark shaped like a dragonfly wing. Mine, dark as a Damson plum, lies flat against my belly; John Willis's hovers near the base of his neck, curved up, as if flying for his chin.

I can't help but wish he looked more like his daddy. At least his hair's the same as Ray's—dirty brown with red glints. They share the same laugh, too—a lighthearted, almost musical sound that tumbles out, free-fall.

If John Willis had been around Ray more, other similarities might have sprouted. It's always good for a boy to see how a man does things, especially when the man's his daddy, but Ray couldn't be there often. He had other obligations.

Though the church women might tell otherwise, I could have married Ray if I'd wanted. He offered to leave Ginny even before John Willis was born, saying he'd move his clothes and woodworking equipment into my trailer that very night, and, soon as he could arrange a divorce, we'd make it legal, changing my name from Grace Cunningham to Grace Ledbetter.

"No." That's what I told him as I reached out touching the stripe of moonlight that silvered our bed sheet, and it wasn't because of any sympathy I felt for his wife that I said it. God knows, though I'm ashamed to admit, I've never felt much of anything for holier-than-thou Ginny in her spotless maroon robe. "Whatever this is between us," I told Ray, "is the best I've ever had with any man. Truly more than I expected. A hundred times better than when I ran off and married Buddy Haskins at sixteen and better than when I left Buddy for Foster Cunningham ten years later. I'm not willing to take chances again, Ray. No use tampering with what feels right."

Reaching up, he cupped my chin in the wide span of his hand. Slowly, with his other hand, he removed the pins that held my dark hair. The only sound, besides the faint ticking of a clock, was his breathing and my own. As he took out the remaining pins, setting free the final strands, I felt suddenly hallowed and peaceful, as if the two of us were in a large church, bathed by multicolored light streaming through stained-glass windows.

I often felt like that with Ray. Never with Buddy Haskins. Never with Foster Cunningham. Only Ray.

Back then Spero wasn't much more than a gas station, an elementary school, two churches, and a combination beauty shop and service station, co-owned by Angelene Johnson and her husband, Jimbo. Because of the smallness of the town, there was no place to hide my swelling belly after John Willis's conception. Right away, the whispers began. At the service station, I could imagine them joking, trying to guess who the father might be between guzzles of Cheerwine. Angelene, pouring rotten-smelling permanent solution and blue-tinted dyes over old women's heads, probably made a soap opera plot of my predicament, and the church women, egged on by Ginny, surely deemed me worthy of hellfire and damnation.

But I never admitted, except to John Willis, that Ray was his daddy. Still they suspected.

Especially Ginny.

"Well?" John Willis asks, holding his cigarette stub up to my face.

"That ropey smelling stuff's illegal. If I wind up in the jailhouse, who'll cook for you?"

He laughs, and I laugh. I thought he'd offer me his cigarette again, but when he doesn't, I pick up his yellowed T-shirt and sour-smelling socks from the sofa and fold the newspaper scattered about on the floor. "You should live better."

"I know."

"It might be those cigarettes making you so careless."

Soon as the words fly from my mouth, he reaches out, touching my shoulder. The hangdog way he looks makes me feel ashamed for acting like his mama even though that's what I am.

"Why, Mama Grace, I'm truly surprised. It's not like you to criticize what you don't know." He turns from me, holding what little's left of his "herbs" daintily between thumb and index finger. I surprise myself by taking the foul thing from him. "Don't I get one of my own?"

"Well Lordy be. Anything you want. Anything atall." As he takes a thin paper out of his tin box, sprinkling it with gray leaves, I almost change my mind. Something doesn't feel right. There's a nag in my head telling me *no.* But ignoring my better judgment, I inhale the old one anyway, then blow out. Lowering myself to John Willis's rag rug, I lean back against the sofa.

I sit there, cross-legged, for the longest while, feeling purely content. Smoking one of my son's funny cigarettes is not a harmful thing to do, I tell myself. A person needs to keep up with what's going on in the world. I've tried kiwi and mangoes. Even tried sushi once, though I almost gagged. Nothing more peculiar than eating raw fish. I close my eyes. When my thoughts backtrack, I think of Ray...

"Hold it," John Willis instructs.

"I am holding it," I say. "See. I'm holding it just like you—between my thumb and the next finger."

"The smoke. Hold the smoke."

With the fresh cigarette, I do as John Willis instructs, leaning back, waiting until my lungs feel pumped up as inner tubes before letting go.

Handing it back, I tell John Willis I feel swimmy-headed.

He laughs. "Maybe you ate too much chicken casserole."

"Any left?"

"Uh-uh. All gone. Want some popcorn?"

"Believe I might."

Before he goes to the kitchen, he hands the cigarette back to me and I get reacquainted. As I study the design on the rug, the blue pieces of cloth begin to grow, joining up with the yellow. Colors have never looked quite so bright before. I wonder if it's what I'm smoking, or my imagination.

Ray told me once, "Why, lady, I bet you could dream up about anything."

He wasn't wrong.

I've always been blessed with visualizing. Yet despite my gift for invention, I could never quite make Ray there when he wasn't. Though I could close my eyes and think it, I could never make it quite the same. No warm imprint of his fingers on my skin. No touch or smell of him—pine shavings mingled with spicy aftershave, and the direct way he had of looking at me, almost as if he knew my thoughts before I had a chance to think them through.

"But I am there, don't you see?" he told me when I tried to explain. "I'm there cause that's where I want to be."

I knew it to be at least partly true.

Even after all these years, he's never left. Not completely. He rarely comes by the trailer anymore, but I still see him—at softball games, in the cabinet shop he owns down on Main or at Phil's Pizza, where I work evenings.

At Phil's he usually orders the salad bar and a bottle of Miller High Life. Because of stomach troubles, he rarely eats pizza anymore.

"How you been doing, Gracie?"

There is something uplifting in the sound of Ray's voice. And I swear, a blaze of pure light radiates from his blue eyes, connecting us still. Sometimes, I even forget that I wait tables and live in a mobile home and that I've never owned a microwave nor traveled any further than Myrtle Beach. All that matters is that Ray sits there, watching as he gives his order, and that I write all the words down in big block letters across my pale green pad.

"How's our boy?" he sometimes asks, if no one's sitting nearby.

Bending my head over my pad, I tell him about the A John Willis made in refrigeration and about those crazy stories he reads, but I never mention that he smokes funny cigarettes. Other times, we speak of an impending storm or fishing conditions over at Piney Lake or all the new construction going on down in Asheboro.

Before our conversation ends, he gets personal: "I'm glad you still wear your hair long," he might tell me, never mentioning how it's now sprinkled with gray. Or, "You have the most delicate hands, Gracie," or he might mention how I've managed to stay slim or the way my cheeks dimple when I smile.

Sometimes, rarely but sweetly, he brings up the past, all the crazy things we used to do. "Still play cowboys and Indians?" After asking, he ducks his head shyly and plain as if it happened that very minute; I envision the snakeskin boots, dyed a soft coral color, he once bought me. Boots with feathers and spurs attached, and him in a black-banded Stetson, never admitting completely to being good or bad.

There was no need to admit. Not to me. I knew the man soul and bone. Every inch. Every scar. Even those that couldn't be seen.

I don't do as well with talking. Sometimes when he's near, I feel too full of the sight of him to remember what I'd intended to say. Sometimes all I manage is, "How you, Ray?"

He grins when I ask. "Just tolerable."

Other times, when I manage to be more talkative, I remind him that I know he is the same, the way he's always been. "Heard you helped out old Miss Cranford," I told him the last time he came by. "Heard you planted her tomatoes. Heard you repaired her rickety fence and painted it bright yellow."

Our conversations form brief wisps of brightness, breaking up the monotony of our lives. And on those days when he does not come, I carry him in my head, recalling conversations, word for word, from a previous time as my worn-out shoes make roads across the restaurant floor.

After we finish our talk, I go about my business, waiting other tables, pouring drinks, refilling shakers with Parmesan, oregano, and hot, dried pepper. The whole while I'm conscious that he's looking at me. When I don't feel the burn of his eyes anymore, I know he's gone.

Later, when I clear his table, I find a ten dollar bill, sticking crisp as celery from the empty beer mug.

I do not need the money, and Ray does not have that much to spare, but I put it in my pocket anyway. That's what he intends. It's part of what we do.

John Willis helps me eat the butter-drenched popcorn. We giggle.

"I ought to be ashamed," I confess, "whiling away the afternoon. I need to be at Phil's by four."

"You work too hard, you know that?"

John Willis's hair sticks up. When I reach out to smooth it down, an odd feeling creeps over me. I suddenly have a fresh suspicion I shouldn't have puffed on those odd-shaped cigarettes. "I'm not sure why I'm doing this," I confess. "I'm certainly old enough to know better."

"You're doing it cause you're a liberated woman. You make your own decisions."

"I'm serious. Maybe I'm just trying to catch up. Maybe I'm just feeling desperate, not wanting the world and its doings to leave me behind. Maybe I'm afraid of getting old, John Willis."

"Never knowed you to be afraid of nothing."

"Maybe that's because I never wanted you to know."

Before I leave, I rinse the bowl that held the chicken casserole, watching khaki-colored sprigs of broccoli dog-paddle for John Willis's drain. There are no paper towels, and the only dishcloth smells sour, so I leave the dish draining on the kitchen counter. "I just might fix apple cobbler tomorrow to go with the macaroni and cheese," I tell him. "Want me to bring some over?"

"You're too good, Mama."

"Earning stars for my crown, that's all."

"Don't fool yourself. Ain't no place for crown wearing. There's only here, only now."

Noticing how solemn he looks, one part of me wishes he didn't believe that way, but another part of me remains proud that he believes however he wants without my interference.

"We all don't think alike," I say to him, sounding puffed up, even to myself, "and the way I think isn't necessarily the way you think."

After I finish my spouting off, I wonder: what do I believe anyway? I halfway know, but it's like stars—bright, shining, yet somehow too distant for proper acquaintance. I've always meant to study on it more, to clarify the fuzzy spots, but being John Willis's mama hasn't left much time for pondering.

At the door, I hug him bye. Because he's greased himself with tropical suntan oil, he smells like fruit salad. Even after I get behind the wheel of my faded-blue Pinto, whiffs of coconut remain in my head.

I turn on the ignition, and find the country station on the radio. I sit there, giving the cloud in my head time to loosen, as I listen to Willie Nelson sing about blue eyes and rain. John Willis's screen door opens. He sticks his head out. I wave to him. I continue to smile at my son as I shift into reverse.

He frowns. He tells me something, but for the life of me I can't make it out.

"What?" I ask, but I suppose he doesn't hear me through the windshield, so I keep backing up.

John Willis comes running then, both arms waving. Too late, I understand. *Stop.* That's been his message. The back wheel of my car humps up. "Lord forgive me," I say out loud.

John Willis rushes to the back of the car, squarely facing the results of my transgression.

"Mercy," I say, dreading that I must get out and look too.

Soon as I get there, I bend and peep beneath the bumper, but all I see is John Willis's hairy arm reaching for whatever I've hit. What he drags out is a blond puppy dog with long, curly ears and a twisted mouth, blood outlining the bared teeth. The animal does not move, not even a twitch. His tongue, hanging sideways from his mouth, resembles a limp ribbon. Then, about the time I've resigned myself to his being dead, he lets out a pitiful howl, and one of his eyes, the iris dark and gloomy, opens.

"Oh, dear Jesus." My hand trembles as I reach for John Willis's arm. My fingers feel numb. "I shouldn't have smoked that cigarette."

"Don't be foolish, Mama. Could've happened to anybody."

He takes me by the arms, wanting me to see the situation his way. "The two aren't connected. The damned dog didn't have sense enough to get out of the way, that's all."

If it hadn't been for that puppy's accusing eyeball, I might've accepted John Willis's explanation. "It's actions and reactions," I say to him, though I'm not completely sure what I mean. "Smoking that cigarette was a sin, at least for me. A voice deep inside told me so, but I went ahead with it anyway."

"Ah-law," John Willis says.

When a couple of blue-tailed flies begin to swarm over the cocker's carcass, John Willis fans them away. He pokes the dog gently with his bare toes. "Still breathing."

The open eye of that hurt animal continues to power-drill through my heart. My son bends down, balancing on the balls of his feet. He touches the dog. When he gets back up, puppy blood covers the palm of his hand. "Back's broken," he says. "Must be all messed up inside. Guess I've got to shoot him."

"We don't even know where he came from. We don't know who he belongs to."

"Don't reckon ownership matters now, Mama. No need to let an animal suffer."

I walk back to the driver's side of the car. My stomach churns. My head aches. Though I try not to think about the cocker, I keep remembering the bright smear of his blood on the pavement.

When John Willis comes out of his apartment, he holds his hunting gun. Purple sunglasses protect his eyes from what he is about to do.

My son, I suppose, is right. Mercy requires that the dog be shot, but I am right too. The animal's death rests on my head.

I do not go with him behind the car. I do not want to see, but when the gun fires twice, I jerk as if the bullets pierce my own skin.

Once back inside the apartment, John Willis brings me a Coca-

Cola. "Now calm yourself, Mama." He speaks gently, places his large hand on my shoulder.

"Now don't be treating me like a child. I'm not tottery yet."

He smiles, kisses my cheek. When he stands straight again, I notice the wing mark decorating his neck. The first time they brought him to me in the hospital, I searched his seven-pound, four-ounce body for something wrong. His head had been round as an orange. Ten fingers and ten pink toes. Nothing missing. Nothing extra. All parts accounted for. No sin marks. Not one single blemish except the tiny, harmless birthmark holding him from perfection. I took it as a sign: God's approval of me and Ray. Only a pencil dot against us.

"The accident happened because of my wrongdoing," I say to John Willis.

"You toked a joint. That's all. What you did has no relation to that dead dog."

"Everything's related," I say to my son, though I doubt he will believe. "Everything's connected. Everything means something."

"Ah-law."

"Do you know what it spells backwards?" I ask him.

"You are just upset."

"Well, go on. Tell me. What does it spell?"

John Willis scratches his head. "What does *what* spell backwards?"

I focus my eyes, my vision making a straight line to him. "*Dog,*" I say, slowly, precisely, so there'll be no mistaking.

Despite his deep summer tan, John Willis pales. He turns away from me. "That's silly, Mama Grace. You're beginning to sound as ridiculous as those church women you're all the time criticizing. That's the way they carry on. They claim if you play rock and roll records backwards, you hear devil messages. They claim to know when the end of the world's going to be and the time they say comes and passes and we're still here and then they come up with some new time. Now they've even come up with a devil brand of washing detergent."

John Willis uses heavy ammunition to dissuade me. He knows I object to the ways of those church women. He, more than anybody, knows the harm they've inflicted on me and his daddy.

"It's not as if I search for meaning," I tell him. "No need searching. It's there in the shape of a thing sometimes, or the way it's spelled, or a sound."

John Willis refuses to let it rest. He keeps blabbering, trying to make what I'd seen not be so. Finally he gives up. "Guess I've got no business arguing with my own stubborn mama, now have I? You ought to know what's right for you, now isn't that so, just like I know what's right for me?"

"Yes, and we shouldn't be trying to confuse one another."

When John Willis grins, I swear, light seems to radiate from him—powerful light, the same light that falls from Ray's eyes.

Soon as I see the light, I know my son will be able to ferret through his own rights and wrongs.

I hug him. "You're natured like your daddy, John Willis, despite whatever peculiar notions and habits you might have."

He ducks his head, grins. His glow becomes my own.

Not a godly glow, mind you, but *goodly*. The same with something extra.

Gradually, the picture of the dead dog, though still stuck in my mind, fades from full color to brown tones.

Photo by Lori Burkhalter-Lackey

The Woven Wall

Kennette H. Wilkes

I have stolen a strand
of the spun gold you wear
so lightly at your heart
and with my tight weaving
constructed a wall between
me and my doomsdays.

I am safe. I can break
my alliance with death
and read theology
in a children's book.

Forget my tales of alienation.
I am engaged in the erotic act
of looking at myself peel
the Bible pages off, verse
by verse.

White Horses

Tricia Lande

The first time I saw Dorothea Lange's photo, *Migrant Woman*, I was ten years old and thought it was a picture of my Aunt Vergie. Aunt Verg, who at forty-five talked to spirits and saw white horses in the night, gutted tuna for a living, pulling her sharp knife upward in the fish's soft underbelly that shined mother-of-pearl under the fish market lights.

The picture of that migrant farm woman was in *Life* or *Look*, one of those photo-heavy magazines so popular in 1941, and I ran with it through the clapboard house I shared with my grandmother and aunt.

Aunt Vergie and Grandma sat on the glassed-in front porch where they always spent their evenings. They would talk quietly, or stare off down our hill toward the west channel of the Los Angeles Harbor. Aunt Verg always curled up on the old black car seat someone had pulled out of a '36 Ford, and my grandma sat in her wooden rocker, where she would fit a light bulb inside a cotton sock, making a hard surface to work her darning needle against, taking small, careful stitches.

My grandma must have heard me coming because she said something like, "fans...silly in November." Then she yelled, "Soody, don't you all let that screen door bang," a second before I pushed through the door, letting it slam behind me.

Then she said, "Sue Donna," as if that was all she needed to say. Sue Donna was my real name, but I was only called that when a family member was irritated with me.

"Look here what I got. Aunt Vergie, you got your picture in a magazine!"

Vergie sat fanning herself. She had a red-and-white fan with a peacock outlined in gold on its face, and I had one just like it. She and I had been given those fans by the Japanese man that owned the only

Chinese restaurant in San Pedro. That was where we lived then—San Pedro, the waterfront area of Los Angeles.

I sat down next to Vergie on that hard seat, laid the magazine across her lap, and she put the fan down on the apple box that served as a coffee table. Vergie stared at that picture for minute, then outlined it with her finger.

"Well, Soody baby, this ain't a picture of me. It looks like me, but it ain't. Hell, she looks like all of the Bybee women."

The woman in the picture held one hand up so that it lightly touched her cheek, and Vergie said, "She even got cotton-picker hands. Look at them scars." The picture was not in color so the marks on the woman's hands showed up as dark blotches as if the film was flawed.

"How do you get cotton-picker hands, Aunt Verg?"

"Get bad scratched from picking cotton. You out in the fields all day you cain't clean the cuts proper, so they don't heal right. That's why I'm glad I got me a different kind of job now."

The marks on my aunt's hands matched those in the picture, only Vergie's were red. On days I had gone to the fish market after school just to be with her, I had watched those scarred hands work. They moved so quickly, scraping the sides of fish with a knife, sending scales flying like a shower of blue-green sequins that turned dull moments later. I could see those scars when Vergie held up the picture to my grandma.

"She looks like us, don't she Momma?"

Grandma pushed her glasses up on her nose and looked at the picture. "Well, let me see the thing, Vergie."

"Yep. Just like a white Indian. Look there, Soody. See, them too-close-together eyes and that little thin nose is what comes from being part Cherokee. That skinny hair," Grandma pulled her own fine white wisps behind her small pink ears, "that's what comes from being Scotch-Irish. Scotch-Irish got terrible bad hair."

Grandma rarely wore her teeth, and she had a habit of pulling her lips inward, rubbing them against her gums before and after she spoke.

That soothed her gums, she once told me, and she did that now.

"Do you think she's kin, Grandma?"

"Probably. Woman's probably from Arkansas so she's probably a Bybee. Bybees married everybody in the whole damned state, then started marrying each other. Whole damned place is related."

The intermarriage of my grandfather's family, a group of people Grandma considered to be completely depraved, was one of her favorite topics of conversation. The truth was that she and my grandfather were also related. But somehow that was different in her eyes because they were related on their mothers' side of the family and their last names were not the same. Usually, she would go on for sometime on this subject of intermarriage, but Vergie stopped her.

Vergie laid the magazine in her lap and began fanning herself again. "I seen a white horse last night."

"You never done that, Vergie."

"Yes I did, Momma. I looked out the window about midnight. And there it come yonder flying through the night sky."

"We left all that back in Arkansas. All the white horses. They don't have no white horses in California."

"Grandma, I seen white horses at the Fourth of July parade. They was real big and they had silver saddles like the Lone Ranger's got."

"Don't mean them kind of white horses. I mean omen white horses. Spirits. Somebody in the family sees a white horse in the night and it means somebody in the family going to pass on. But them spirit horses stay in the country. They don't go by salt water. It makes them dissolve."

Grandma leaned across me as if being closer to Vergie would help her get her point across. "That's why you cain't see no white horses in California."

"Well, you didn't let me finish, as usual, Momma. It was a white horse, but it was a white sea horse and it was swimming through the sky. Its tail was curling and uncurling and it was just streaming along."

Grandma leaned back in her chair, rocking twice as fast as before. "Soody, I want you to mind what's being said here, because this is just what comes from cousins marrying each other for about five generations.

It makes the kids, and grandkids, and their kids peculiar. That's just what's wrong with the Roosevelts. Eleanor and Franklin is cousins. Then they raised all them peculiar kids and him getting the paralysis and all."

By now Vergie was fanning just as fast as my grandmother was rocking.

"I want to know something, Vergie. And I want a straight answer. Where did you all get that fan?" Grandma rubbed her lips against her gums.

"I want her to tell more about them sea horses," I said.

"I don't want no more nonsense about no sea horses. I want to know about that fan."

"You know damned well where I got the fan. Hiro give it to me at the restaurant."

"The child's got one just like it. You taking the child with you when you meeting this man?"

"We didn't meet him. We just gone in for lunch. He give them away to everybody what goes in for lunch."

"I don't want you taking Soody in there again. Feeding a child fish heads is a shameful thing, Vergie."

"I didn't eat no fish heads, Grandma."

"Man ain't got no sense anyway. Whoever heard of a Japanese man owning a Chinese restaurant. Don't make no sense."

Vergie fanned harder. "He tried running a Japanese restaurant, but folks around here is ignorant about Japanese food and they wouldn't come in."

"Folks around here know enough not to eat fish heads."

"Jesus, Momma." And with that Vergie got up and stomped off into the house, taking her fan with her.

My grandmother and I sat on the porch for a time longer, listening to the sound of a tug whistle in the channel, a lonesome long sound that was carried up the hill by the wind. With it came the dead fish smell from the canneries on Terminal Island, that listless sandbar that sits in the middle of the harbor. Finally, my grandmother moved her lips together twice, and said, "This ain't going to turn out well."

The next day was a Sunday, my aunt's one day off a week. The two of us always spent that day together—I should say the three of us, because we would see Hiro Ikeda on Sundays.

Sundays, Vergie would braid my blond hair, weaving red or pink ribbons through the plaits, and she would put on her soft green dress with large white polka dots and wear white cotton gloves on her small hands, rubbing the red scars with lotion first. We would walk down the hill to the wharf, passing bridal shop windows with mannequins in long white dresses. Past bars with peeling signs that said names like Longfellow's and Shanghai Red's. Women stood at the bars' entrances wearing gaudy black dresses trimmed with shiny sequins. Those women, their heavy faces made up in white, would smile at me with maroon lips. Vergie would say, "Soody, they ain't bad women, really. Just lonely inside. You do sad things when you're lonely inside."

As we walked, my aunt told me stories about her only sister, my long-dead mother, or about how things had been back in Arkansas when my family left ten years before. The story she told most often was the one about my great-great-grandfather, and the telling never varied.

"He didn't want to go in the army, Soody. Didn't want to go in no man's army, blue or gray. But the gray coats come and got him. Said, 'Boy, we going shoot you for sure if you don't join up,' and him madder than a hen at Sunday dinner. They made him build bridges. Built bridges all across Georgia. Well, he built them bridges all right. But just as soon as one got built, it got blowed up and burnt down during the night, one after another. All his gray coat officers, they never could figure out how the hell them Union soldiers was sneaking across their lines to burn down them bridges. Them crackers never did figure it out." Vergie would laugh as if she had been a part of my great-great-grandfather's scheme.

And I would always ask, "But if he blowed up and burnt all them bridges how did he get back home?" Vergie would shake her head and say, "Soody baby, you got to learn to dream."

But that particular November morning, the last Sunday in that cold month, she didn't tell any of her usual stories as we passed those wooden brides in the store windows, or the washed-out women dressed in black, but said she had seen the white horse again the night before.

"It come streaking through the sky and its hooves pounding against nothing, but sending up sparks just the same."

"I thought you said it was a sea horse. Sea horses got no hooves to pound."

"I only said that to get on Momma's nerves." Vergie pulled her gray cloth coat closed at her throat. "Her and her hissy fits. She don't believe nothing I say anyway."

"That's because sometimes you tell wrongful stories, Aunt Vergie. Like how we come to get them fans."

"Lord, Sue Donna. You getting just like her. You all want to hear the rest of it about the horse or not?" Then she went on as if I had said yes.

"You know who was on the back of that horse? It was your Momma, Modene Folton. Modene Folton, big as life and wearing a long flowing dress. She says to me, 'Vergie, it gets real lonesome sometimes.' It's an omen for sure, Soody."

Vergie's voice trailed off at the end. Then she was quiet, and no matter what I asked she said no more until we reached the docks.

Hiro Ikeda stood on the wharf, which smelled of creosote and diesel fuel from the tugboats docked nearby. His small white launch with its blue-and-white striped canopy was there too, lightly bouncing against a pylon. That launch was always clean, its white paint perfect. He took great care with the little boat and was as gentle with it as he was with my aunt.

It was overcast and cool that morning, and Hiro wore his navy-blue pea coat. He was a small man, no bigger than my aunt, and when he wore that pea coat with the collar turned up it hid even his nose, so that it seemed he looked at the world peering from a shell, checking to make sure things were safe before he completely emerged.

Hiro was just a kind little gray-haired man who drank lemon tea and ate steamed dumplings—vegetables wrapped in dough and drenched in sweet, thick honey sauce. To hear him tell it, nothing ever happened in his small life of work and sleep. Nothing more than a storm now and then that would blow up from Baja, and the three of us in his launch would ride the swells while Hiro gripped the small boat's wheel as if it were all there was between us and eternity.

I don't know how long Vergie and Hiro had been meeting for these Sunday launch rides, only that it had been going on as long as I could remember, and they always took me with them. That morning they greeted each other as they always did. Vergie held out her cotton-gloved hand—I never saw her remove those gloves when he was around—he took it in his small brown fingers, and bowed slightly at the waist. "I am happy to see you, Vergie." He always said it in a way that made it seem there was some doubt she would come.

Vergie, who could string enough four-letter words together to make a sailor blush, smiled and softly said, "Thank you, Hiro. It's so nice that you all asked us."

Then, as always, Hiro repeated the ritual with me, taking my hand and saying, "Little Miss Soody. You look so sweet today." He touched my hair so softly that it seemed more like the touch of a gentle breeze.

The sea was smooth that morning, and it did not take long to reach the rocks of the breakwater. We dropped anchor just inside the harbor so I could watch the fat seals that lay on the gray boulders, and the pelicans that would glide so low their bellies seemed to skim the water's surface. This was my favorite part of our voyage because Hiro would let me sit at the wheel.

Vergie and Hiro sat in the back of the boat, each wrapped in a blanket, speaking softly. Hiro said, "We could try, Vergie. If we just tried."

"Where would we live? Ain't nowhere we could live in peace. Then there's the child. I got the child to think about."

"You know how I feel about the child, Virginia. Besides, it's too late to have our own."

"It ain't too late just yet, Hiro." And my aunt laughed what sounded to me a young girl's laugh, light and soft like my friends at school. "But then we'd be in a real fine mess for sure, having a mixed-blood baby." Then she laughed again, but this time she didn't sound young at all. "Well, Momma's always yelling about the misery of family marrying family. Guess she wouldn't have nothing to yell about on our account."

Vergie said no more for a minute, then, "I got to think on it some."

"Vergie, we don't have half a lifetime left, and it seems like that's how long you've been thinking about this." It was the first time I had ever heard anger in Hiro's voice. After that he moved away from Vergie, came forward near where I sat and leaned over the railing.

I looked at him over my shoulder, and I could see that Hiro Ikeda was crying. Not loudly; there were no sobs, no deep throaty sounds. Just large drops of water that hung on his cheeks. We came home early that Sunday, Hiro and Vergie not speaking on the way in, and Vergie silent on our walk back up the hill.

That next Sunday, for the first time in my memory, Vergie and I did not go out in Hiro Ikeda's launch. That Sunday was December 7, 1941. That day Vergie Bybee cried and my grandmother rocked in her wooden chair, but did not darn socks.

The following Sunday Vergie did not put on her soft green dress, but a black one. She braided my hair, but did not weave pink ribbons into the plaits. She did not wear her white gloves, but held that red-and-white fan with the gold peacock on its face in her bare hand as we walked down the hill to the center of town and stood on the sidewalk with a crowd of other people.

A flatbed truck with wooden stakes around the sides of its bed sat idling in the street. Hiro stood in the midst of fifteen or so other Japanese men at the back of the truck, their belongings tied in white sheet bundles at their feet. There were other men too. Large white men in dark suits and wide brimmed hats. Vergie and I watched them as they yelled orders at the Japanese. We watched as they shoved this one and that. As they demanded that the small brown people climb onto the truck, Aunt Vergie leaned into me.

The crowd on the sidewalk yelled too. "Hang them! Send them to hell! Sneaky bastards!"

When Hiro climbed aboard the truck, Vergie held the closed fan over her head, not high, but just inches above her light brown hair. If Hiro saw her signal he gave no sign, but settled against the back of the truck cab and stared off toward the channel.

The truck filled with men and belongings tied into bundles and moved off down the street. Vergie said, "We ain't going see him again, Soody." And even at that young age, I knew that to be true.

I ran across that picture, *Migrant Woman*, last summer. It was in a book, *Collected Works of Depression Era Art.* I looked again at the picture of that stick-thin woman with fine brown hair parted in the middle, pulled back behind tiny ears peeling from too much sun. I saw the way her scarred hand lightly touched her cheek, and that look in her eyes which haunts me. Far off, as if she could not stand seeing what was in front of her. Her small mouth, lips, made straight by anguish.

In that picture I see the image of my aunt, see her scrape at the sides of those tuna with their sequin scales that turned dark over time. And I think about how it must have been for Vergie on that hard-edged day when she could no longer dream, and decided there would be no more for her than putting that sharp knife in a fish's underbelly, pulling it upwards so that what gave the creature life spilled out on a hard white metal tray.

Photo by Jude Keith

October Fire

Bettie M. Sellers

In the churchyard, flames, the Burning Bush,
a maple touched to fire, by autumn fanned.
Were I possessed as Moses was, the hush
might speak, Jehovah's voice resound. I stand
uncertain, questions wrinkling my face:
Should I kneel, is this some holy ground?
Or is it just the usual for this place
that maples turn, a season come around?
And as I ponder, November rain
gathers wind from lowering eastern skies
to strip the maple of its leaves. The stain
of scarlet filters down before my eyes.
I wait too long; I watch the moment pass
till only ashes stir upon the grass.

One Last Time

Lori Russell

"I want to go back to Yosemite one last time," Mac said looking at me with eyes the color of his faded-blue hospital gown. His skin pulled taut over his cheekbones like yellow leather. Silver and black whiskers sprouted on the ridge of his jaw. "Well, what do you think, Doris?"

I stared at the green plastic tubing that wound from Mac's nose over his ears to a socket in the wall. It hissed a constant exhale of oxygen. How much time had passed since the doctor met with us? Five minutes? An hour? I pressed my fingernails deep into the flesh of my palm. White half-moons appeared on the skin under my nail tips, but I felt nothing. "OK, Mac. If you think you can make it to Yosemite, let's do it."

Mac's thin fingers reached for the plastic basin beside him. His shoulders shuddered as he retched. Then, wiping his chin with a tissue, he whispered, "When do we leave?"

We first came to Yosemite on our honeymoon. Money was tight then, so we stayed in a cabin and ate boxed cereal and milk for breakfast. Each morning I hiked to the bathroom with a terry cloth robe pulled tight over my new lingerie. We packed picnic lunches and spent the days hiking the trails above Tuolomne Meadows and Wolf Creek. At night, we watched from the valley floor as the rangers pushed a huge bonfire off one of the nearby cliffs. The embers cascaded in a fiery waterfall.

When the kids were small, we had camped out each summer in a canvas tent that smelled of mildew, and rolled out our four sleeping bags on air mattresses. Mac and I always zipped our bags together because I loved sleeping next to him, feeling the warmth of his skin and the curve of his hip against me. Mac taught Kathy and Jim how to thread a pink salmon egg on a hook and fish for trout in the Merced River. When the fish weren't biting, we'd ride our bikes through the redwood groves on the valley floor.

Mac and I returned to the cabins after Kathy and Jim left home. By then, they had been remodeled to include a bathroom and shower. That was as much luxury as Mac would allow. I'd always wanted to stay at the Wawona Lodge at the south end of the park. I imagined sitting in the shade of the pines watching the people. Mac thought I was crazy. Some things just weren't worth the fight.

It was a Thursday in late October when we left for Yosemite this time, one of those warm golden autumn mornings when the sky is bluer than you ever thought possible. The leaves of the apple tree had begun to curl around the last of the red-skinned fruit and the dew was still wet on the ivy.

I packed the car: the thermos of coffee for me and the wicker basket we once filled with dry salami and Swiss cheese for Mac. Today it carried Gerber's strained carrots and chocolate pudding, a can of high-protein strawberry-flavored liquid, and some crackers. Mac had lost his appetite for most foods.

He watched me from the porch chair.

"Put the suitcases in first," he commanded as I opened the trunk. I hoisted his beige leather case first, then my blue Samsonite.

"Doesn't fit with both of them," I called.

"Yes it does. Jiggle the blue one until it fits in the back."

I shoved hard against the case, then bounced it up and down. It wedged on top of the spare tire. The leather case slid in easily.

In the backseat I put the bag of Mac's pills: one for nausea, another for diarrhea; morphine, sleeping pills, pills for agitation, and heart and blood pressure medication.

Mac shuffled to the car. He stood for a moment, hooked his cane on the door, and fell back onto the front seat. Slowly he picked up his left leg with both hands and slung it into the car. His breath was quick, his upper lip shone with sweat. Picking up his other leg, he heaved it into the car.

I slid onto the seat easily and turned the ignition key. Mac had driven on all of our vacations. It was one of those unspoken agreements we made in marriage, like who made the morning coffee and who bought the stamps. Since Mac had started chemo, I'd been driving more. He just didn't feel up to it. I'd also been doing all the grocery shopping and errands, jobs Mac had readily accepted when he retired. My usually generous husband reveled in seeking out bargains and triple coupon savings. But now, six T-bone steaks and eight chickens lay thick with white frost in the freezer. Mac had lost his taste for meat about a month ago.

The traffic was light leaving the city.

"Look at the new condos," Mac said, pointing to the cluster of white stucco buildings with red-tiled roofs by the curve of the freeway. The condos had actually been built about the time Mac began treatments but for the last year he had only gone between the house and the hospital.

We rode on in silence. Red tipped the branches of the trees as if the color came to the ends first and worked its way inward toward the trunk. The car strained as we drove up to the pass. The brown hills were patched with black where the grass had been burned.

I didn't know what it was to lose a husband. I had watched friends go through it, watched them hang on to every shred of hope, seeing only what they wanted to see. I wished I could have been that way. Instead I saw Mac's every change: the luster in his eyes dulled by medication, the dark hollows of his cheeks, the pale yellow of his skin. His stomach had started to swell, like a pregnant woman's. Sometimes he became so short-winded he had to stand up to draw a full breath. He was filling up with his own body fluid, the doctor said. Drowning.

I placed my hand on his leg. It was thin like a child's, the kneecap bony and angular in my hand.

"Remember when we used to stop and buy a block of ice for your feet?" Mac asked as the car eased downhill from the pass. "That was when we had the old green Chevy."

"And no air-conditioning!" I laughed, remembering how it had been hot on our other trips through the valley. Wrapping the ice in a towel, I had rested my feet on top of the block and stayed cool.

I followed the Airstream trailer in front of us down the two-lane highway past plowed fields. The earth had been turned upside down and large clods of dirt lay drying in the sun. A lone patch of cornstalks stood tall like yellowed bristles of a toothbrush. There was so much brown this time of year. The hills were dark like the tanned back of a field hand.

I had hoped for autumn color—gold, orange, crimson, cinnamon—like at home, but here there was only an occasional rusty-needled pine to add some color. Abandoned cars decayed under trees and against fence posts. Roadside signs beckoned: Almonds, Pumpkins, Mexican Curios for Sale. We passed knee-high ceramic ducks, skunks, and teddy bears standing in neat rows waiting to be purchased.

"Remember when we came through here and got that flat tire?" I said to Mac. "Kathy was just a baby."

"Yeah, I walked five miles down the road to the gas station. God, it was hot." He rolled down the window and stuck out his hand, testing the air like water in a bathtub. "I don't think it's as hot today." He turned toward me. "Doris, I don't care what else you do, but after I'm gone, buy yourself a fancy car, OK?"

"Right, Mac...like a Mercedes or BMW? Honey, that's just not me, you know that."

"How do I know that? We've always had to worry about money, for the kids, the house, whatever. With the money from the life insurance policy you can get what you want."

I gripped the steering wheel. How could he sit there talking about my life after he is gone? Of course we had talked about this before; what married couple hadn't? But those conversations were theoretical musings made when we were both healthy, when cancer was something that happened to other families and "until death do us part" seemed a romantic notion.

Mac coughed into a yellow-stained handkerchief. His body seized as he exhaled, then was still. Seconds passed. Tears poured down his pink cheeks. He drew a rattled breath and coughed again.

"Slow deep breaths Mac, slow down," I said, grabbing his shoulder. He breathed slowly and the yellow color returned to his face. I pulled off the road. Mac closed his eyes and pressed his head back into the seat. I heard him exhale slowly.

"I'm OK."

"I'll find a place to stop and get something to eat. Give you a chance to get out of the car for a while."

He nodded.

As we approached the next town, I pulled into the parking lot of the Pine Cone Restaurant. I held his arm as he struggled out of the car. Inside, we sat down at a red Formica-topped table. I rummaged through my sack and pulled out a fat pill bottle.

"Take one of these before you eat anything."

He waved me away with the back of his hand. "I don't feel nauseated. I don't even feel hungry."

"Mac, please. The doctor said you're supposed to take them before every meal, you know that."

"I hate these things," he said, pushing two small white pills into his mouth.

"What can I get for you two today?" said the waitress who was now standing beside Mac.

"I'll have the cheeseburger—no onions, fries, and a Diet Coke."

"And what about you, sir?" she continued, flashing a wide smile at Mac.

"Nothing thanks. I brought my own food." He nodded toward the canned protein drink and strained carrots I was pulling from the wicker basket.

"OK. Ma'am, that cheeseburger will be just a few minutes."

I leaned back into the chair. My shoulders felt stiff and sore. A throbbing pain had lodged over my eyes. "Mac, remind me you need your morphine before we leave."

I put the bottle on the table next to the salt-and-pepper shakers. The waitress returned with my Diet Coke.

"I thought you could use these," the waitress said to Mac. She placed a bowl, glass, and silverware in front of him. "For that gourmet meal of yours," she said smiling. "Now all of our customers are going to want what you're having."

Mac's mouth softened into a grin. "Thanks."

She nodded and walked behind the counter to pick up two plates from under the cone-shaped warming lights.

"I'll be back in a minute, honey," I said, and walked toward the back wall to the rest room. Inside, I leaned against the cool white tile. In the reflection of the mirror I saw my wrinkled blue sweatshirt and jeans. Caring for Mac left me no time to worry about what clothes I wore. My skin looked gray and my cheeks sagged into jowls. The circles under my eyes had become darker. How long had it been since I'd slept through the night?

The waitress served my food as I returned, then lined up the ketchup, mustard, and relish jars with the morphine bottle on the table.

"Anything else I can get you?"

I ate in silence while Mac took an occasional bite of the chocolate pudding or a sip of protein drink. After paying the waitress, I took Mac's arm. I held tight to him as we walked to the car.

As we continued, the land spread out between the houses until barbed-wire fences were the only divisions. I followed the telephone poles, giant wooden crosses strung together with wire. We passed through several small towns, each with a liquor store and single gas pump.

After an hour I pulled the car onto the gravel shoulder. "OK, time for your morphine," I said reaching behind Mac's seat for the paper bag that held the medicine.

Mac's eyelids fluttered but didn't open.

I sorted through the plastic containers. Where was the morphine? I counted the bottles...four. There had been five when we left the house. I opened my purse: wallet, Doublemint gum, Kleenex, lipstick. Then I remembered the bottle sitting on the table in the diner. "Mac, did you pick up the morphine off the table?"

"What?"

"At the restaurant, did you pick up the morphine bottle off the table?"

"No." He rubbed his eyes then yawned.

"Damn! Well, it's not here."

"You forgot the morphine?" His eyes widened. "Doris, how could you?"

"I forgot because I'm taking care of everything. Everything Mac. Every pill, every meal, the driving, you, everything. Can't you help with just one little thing like the morphine?" I clenched the wheel and stared straight ahead.

"No. I'm sorry, but I can't."

His words hit me like a slap. I turned toward him stunned. Tears flooded his eyes.

"Damn it, Doris, I can't remember anything anymore. Half the time I don't know if it's day or night. I just wake up, take the next pill, and go back to sleep. I hate it." He pressed his lips together as if trying to stop the flow of words.

"I know you can't help it," I said, beginning to cry. "It's just so much to deal with . . . to see you this way." I slumped against Mac's shoulder. How many tears had I held in during the chemotherapy sessions—the loss of hair, the vomiting, the suppositories, the pain. I hated the way we endlessly tracked every bodily function, and then waited—for the next side effect, the treatment to stop, the inevitable death. Was this all there was?

"I don't want you to go. You just can't die," I said sniffling. "I'm sorry, I've tried to be strong, be the good wife, but it's not fair. It's just not fair." My sobs erupted again, rushing out and echoing off the car windows.

"I'm here with you now, Doris," Mac said softly. His body began to shake.

The sound of muffled cries filled the car. I didn't know where Mac left off and I began. All I felt was warmth as I slumped into his lap. Our breaths rose and fell together. I wanted him to assure me things would be all right, that I would be all right after he was gone. He said nothing.

Mac fished a handkerchief out of his pocket and handed it to me. "Let's just forget the morphine."

"Come on, Mac, you know we can't do that."

"Why can't we? Why can't we just leave it behind, leave all the pills and the cancer too?"

I kissed his neck. "Because it's a part of you now, a part of us. We can't get away from it."

I turned the car around and headed back toward the diner.

As I entered, our waitress, standing behind the cash register, smiled warmly. She held up the brown bottle, shaking it so I could hear the morphine tablets rattle.

"Got 'em right here," she said. "How far did you get?"

"About an hour out of town. Thank you so much. I don't know what we would have done if I couldn't find them."

"Your husband's really sick, isn't he?" She looked straight into my eyes. I remembered the way she had placed the silverware in front of Mac as if he had been a paying customer. I wanted to tell her.

"Yes. He has cancer. We're on our way to Yosemite so he can see it for the last time."

I searched her face for the familiar pained expression I'd seen when we had told our friends of Mac's condition. I expected the words of false hope I'd heard from our families.

"I'm so sorry," she said quietly. "How terrible for you." The lines around her eyes softened. She reached across the counter and placed her hand over mine. It felt warm and moist as if she had just taken it out of the dishwater.

"I lost my husband two years ago. Thought I was going to die right along with him . . . but I didn't." She squeezed my hand gently. "It won't always hurt this bad."

I began to cry.

"Do you want to sit down for a while? I'll get you a cup of coffee."

"No, we're already late. We won't get into the park until after dark and Mac needs his medicine."

"I'll fix you a cup for the road then. It's on the house."

When I returned to the car Mac's eyes were closed. I touched his shoulder.

"How about that morphine?" he said. "I'm hurting." He took the pills with a slurp of coffee and was snoring before we reached the town limits.

I rolled down my window and tuned the radio to the local country western station. There was something about a long drive that made me crave songs about wayward love and big rigs. Mac liked classical music and occasionally some jazz. Usually he'd howl if I turned on a "hick station" as he called it, but since he'd been taking the morphine, he could sleep through anything. I edged the volume up a little higher.

Shadows lengthened on the red rock beneath the manzanita bushes as we drove into the foothills. Gray-green spikes of grass grew in clumps along the side of the road. I pushed down on the accelerator hoping to make up for the time we had lost. The car's engine strained, lurched as it shifted into another gear, then settled back into a soft hum. As I braked around yet another turn I realized there was no quick way to drive through the mountains. Lost time was just that . . . lost.

The sun shone in my rearview mirror. I watched it drop into a pool of orange beyond the edge of the valley. Ahead of me the sky was washed in lavender and the plants became dark silhouettes on the landscape.

Mac moaned softly, folded his arms across his chest and then was quiet. I hummed to the music on the radio as I drove. Finding my way to the park was easier than I had expected. Maybe I would come again someday and stay at the Wawona Lodge. I could sit on the lawn wearing my straw hat and peer over the edge of a fat book at the golfers and tourists. At night I would sit at a corner table in the restaurant and watch the faces of the couples in the candlelight. I'd wear that green dress with the pink roses Mac thought was too gaudy.

I looked over at Mac. Could he read my thoughts? Did he know I was fantasizing about being alone? He lay next to me sleeping softly.

I drove on until we reached the entrance to the park. A short man with wire-rimmed glasses shone a flashlight into the car.

"You folks know your way?"

"Yes," I said, then stopped. Mac had always driven during the daylight. As a passenger, I hadn't paid much attention to how to get to the cabins. "Can you just tell me how to get to Yosemite Village?"

"Follow the signs. You can't miss it." He handed me a map. "Just in case."

I drove along the pine-fringed roads, following the beam of the headlights. Pinholes of light dotted the dark curtain of sky. The cloudy trail of the Milky Way spread out before me. I felt giddy from the smell of pine and dried leaves, excited about greeting an old friend. The road turned gently downward toward the valley. I pushed on the accelerator and we rushed into a tunnel bored through the granite. The car tires thumped and whined. As we emerged from the mountain, the white moon greeted us. It hung round and complete over the valley. I stopped the car, pulled Mac's down jacket from the backseat and got out of the car quietly. At the edge of the road, the valley spread out before my feet. I saw the pewter crest of Half Dome and the steely ridges of the canyon walls in the moonlight.

Mac's jacket smelled of him. I pulled it around me like a warm hug. We had returned to the beauty of the park, to our memories. For Mac, it was the last visit. I would come back again and again. Spreading my arms I embraced the wind as it swept over me. I breathed in, tasting the freshness of the air in my mouth. Looking into the face of the moon I saw no pain, no suffering. I watched until my ears ached and my toes felt numb in my sneakers.

Mac opened his eyes when I slid into the seat next to him.

"Mac honey, we're here. Look. We made it."

Photo by Lori Burkhalter-Lackey

Photo by Marianne Gontarz

It Is Enough

Ruth Daigon

It is enough to lean against
the fabric of your flesh.
It is enough to lie
in the domestic morning.
It is enough to watch light
expand through windows—
rising and falling
between our bodies on this bed,
this room, this continent.

We grow wise watching leaky faucets,
faded wallpaper, mismatched socks.
The coffee boiling on the stove
prepares us for the network news,
shopping malls, miracle cures
and tomorrow always sitting on our bed.

But in this rush of years,
we have not lost the pure imagined past,
the here-it-is, the pitch, the pinnacle
of time shining from within a million
summers or the music so intense   it disappears.

We invent a lifetime out of small things,
free the air between our fingers,
diagram the stars   dream them into
daylight and admit the future
which is here   always here
like a clock that runs forever.

Photo by Marianne Gontarz

Five Years Later

Maril Crabtree

To a Former Lover from a Married Woman

What can I say to you,
who loved the unknown bits and
pieces of me into being
and watched the fragments
weave themselves into another
whole with no more room
for a divided love?

The warp and woof of my
existence lie now
in my own hands,
steadier and wiser with the
passage of my inner time,
knowing more now of what I
chose than when I chose it.

Yes, I would choose again
the same end, but in a
different way, not out of
desperation and the need
to cling to clarity, but out of
freedom and the need to find
my own soul's fabric.

The beginning?
I would not change
a single breathless moment
nor do I fail to savor
all the sharpened memories of it
this hot July night.

Praying in the Dark

Gailmarie Pahmeier

For James Whitehead

Having gone alone to her hotel room after the conference,
an aging professor suffers through her prayers:

Lord, forgive me my common
dreams, my daily deceptions.
Forgive that I have feigned to bless
those books that give me bread,
that I have written save few words
which shine with any soul,
that I have somehow earned a place
solid, certain, removed from blood,
hunger and heart.
Forgive that I no longer have to pray.

And Lord, forgive me my love of the boy,
the one who sings the country songs
with clarity and calm,
the one who reads every book I recommend,
the boy whose memory holds my poems
in place.
Lord, if you can forgive me this, protect him.
I promise to pray again. Amen.

Amen.

A Weaver

Barbara L. Thomas

 Once
contemplated
   a disturbing
       fray
    before
choosing the

 way
the pattern
    should continue
        She
     taught
the shuttle

 symmetry
and rose from
   the loom
       clothed in
    beauty of her
own

 fashioning

Orchards and Supermarkets

Rina Ferrarelli

1.

My thumb doesn't leave a dent
in the avocado.
The undersides of the bananas
are still green. The pears,
Bosc and Bartlett,
have the hardness and heft of rocks.

I stare at the grapes, I look
at the price. The higher it is,
the more sour they are.
I turn a bag of red Delicious
over and over in my hands
looking for a yellow cast.

It's either too soon
or too late,
and I wait, defer, make-do.
Was it always like this,
or have I learned patience at last?

Or is this what wisdom ever was,
being happy with what you can have,
when you can have it?

2.

If I found myself in an orchard,
would I know, did I ever know,
how to pick the fruit
right off the branches?
Would I recognize
the color of ripeness,
the aroma?

But what orchard, what plantation
would ever do?
I want apples and pomegranates,
cherries and pears, oranges
and plums, each kind
suspended in its own season.
It would have to be
a garden of delights.

Divorce

Ellin Carter

Trailing fingers in cool grass
she considers the delicate spirea,
its old names—the bridal wreath,
hardhack and meadowsweet—this tracery
and desiccation after all.

Over her head a pear tree in full
noisome bloom whispers in Middle
English of "The Merchant's Tale,"
of *blisse in marriage,* how beauty
and decay may intertwine.

Then, rising, she lifts up a branch
to carry indoors to the fireplace,
where sparks will kindle quickly, for
pear is the most ardent wood, and white
or green will wither and blaze forth.

Vietnam

Jennifer Lagier

For David

For a decade
we took Da Nang and Cua Tung to bed,
rubbed napalm over shrapnel scars,
calling it love.
For the first two years,
I held you through the nighttime sweats
which scattered hot opiate hallucinations,
fragging holes in your sleep.
Till hostilities went guerrilla.
While the decoy stayed topside,
terrorism tunneled deep underground
and I wore Vietnam like a totem
in this Hanoi Hilton
we built for ourselves,
becoming your hooch mama,
accepting all aggressions,
until Cambodia imploded inside my mouth
and was no longer contained.
Banging my head,
I kamikazied against
your stark white barrack walls,
slipped and ran,
refugee free,
through the dead marriage mud.

Getting On with It

Grace Butcher

When the heart stops oozing blood
& the outpouring is clear as water
(so to speak) then you know you've
turned the corner & will be well.
When you look inward & all the pathways
are no longer dark but clearly lighted
& shine like transparent drinking straws
then you know you'll find your way alone.
When the gray morning has nothing to do
with you & doesn't weigh you down
like a heavy blanket, then you know
that moving will be easy again and
your body will flow through time
like the river it really is, smooth & deep,
no rocks, no shallows to smash or catch you,
keep you from moving on.   When the heart slows
to its normal rhythm and the beauty
of birdsong at dawn doesn't make you cry
because you are alone listening, then you
know that everything has happened that is
going to for now, and you can get on with
your life & everything about it that was
yours alone and always finer than
anyone could ever imagine it would be
without him.

Cauliflower Beach

Carol Schwalberg

They met at Christmas over a goose.

She remarked on his teeth.

He blinked in reply.

She told him to call her when he needed crew on his boat.

A week later, he invited her to watch whales on land.

They had their first dinner in a shopping center four blocks from her house. He sipped martinis before his steak, she mentioned liking wine but he ordered none.

He thought that she was small and had electric hair.

She considered him a mountain of a man, twice her weight and over a head taller. His navy blazer was fine, but his white shirt needed bleach, ironing, and a necktie.

Fearing to be rude, he stared ahead without looking at her and sketched his life story. Missouri-born and Texas-bred, he was a widower without children and a homeowner without a mortgage. He explained that he was an engineer who tested fixtures on spacecraft, which explained nothing at all.

Looking at his profile, she expanded on her work history and skimped on her personal life. A fourth-generation New Yorker, she had zipped from art school to art direction and later drifted into free-lance design and illustration, becoming a visual Jill-of-all-trades. She mentioned divorcing a minor talent with major neuroses, but omitted anything about falling in love with a series of the same. Nor did she say that in Los Angeles, she had twice set up housekeeping with marginal misfits.

Four years before, she had resolved to seek out men who were both sane and solvent. She had found dates who met these requirements, but her times with them seemed the dreariest of her life. Just two weeks before, she had met a friend's reject, a widowed stock market analyst from the Beverly Hills flats. The man sat in her living room for an hour detailing the reasons he was not mourning his wife, a depressive who might go months without speaking. Characterizing himself a paragon of mental health, he nevertheless insisted that any restaurant they selected must be on the near side of Lincoln Boulevard, for he could rarely bring himself to cross major streets.

Tonight, Frank had chosen the very same restaurant as the stock analyst, and he also was saying he did not mourn his wife. When the check came, Annie thought to forestall a list of his wife's failings by suggesting a turn around the shopping center.

Frank smiled, "I've gone to London and Paris, but I've never toured a shopping center before."

After the third shoe store, the stout engineer drew to a halt, "You mean there's more?"

When she nodded, he said, "Next time we have to be brave and cross Lincoln Boulevard."

The stock analyst again, Annie thought, and flashed a look of absolute horror.

"That's a joke," he said. "We can go anywhere you like."

Annie laughed.

They ambled on, Frank joking and Annie laughing, at one point stopping dead in her tracks to double over. Whee, I'm having fun, she thought.

Frank deposited her back on her doorstep at ten-thirty. "I'm baby-sitting a test," he remarked enigmatically. "Seven days a week. Whoo, but am I tired!"

The next Saturday, he turned up wearing the same navy blazer and unironed shirt, but carrying a large package. "I had some tea I wasn't using."

Tea? She reserved tea for advanced stomachaches.

True to his promise, they crossed Lincoln Boulevard to dine at a mediocre but expensive restaurant. By this time, Annie realized that Frank was impervious to hints, and when he ordered his martini, bluntly asked for wine.

He responded with grace. "You know, I've hardly dated at all these last few years. I guess I'm not acting civilized."

He started to make her laugh almost instantly. Once again, he never looked her way and took her home by ten-thirty, without so much as brushing her lips.

The following Saturday, he arrived at the dot of six-thirty, carrying a skillet. A second-hand skillet? Open packages of tea? He must be cleaning house.

They returned to the same steak house. He announced that he would be going to Paris in the middle of February. "I've got to buy clothes!" He sounded so emphatic she could hear the exclamation point.

"You do need clothes," she agreed, not trying to be sarcastic.

"Yes, I have to maintain my position as a fashion leader."

They laughed together and the following Saturday, he arrived in a gray tweed Norfolk jacket. "Handsome," she said. "What else?"

"That's it."

Clothes, one jacket? Annie was puzzled.

This time, when he said good night, he kissed her lightly. She hugged him in response and invited him to dinner the following Saturday. "I'll ask the Creamers, too. I never paid them back for Christmas dinner."

"I'll come at four to help," Frank promised.

He showed up at three-thirty.

In the middle of dressing and running late as usual, Annie threw on a robe and tied the sash carelessly. Frank noticed a flash of bra and inferred that she must like him.

After Annie finished dressing, Frank perched on a stool in the kitchen while Annie sliced and diced, sautéed and simmered. He never made a move to help. Why did he come early, she wondered.

Annie had thought to give of herself and prepare a dish her father's family had brought from Hungary. She thus turned dinner into disaster. Ian Creamer proved allergic to paprika, Janine could not abide sour cream, and Frank picked out each piece of green pepper. "They're against my religion," he said by way of joke, but to put a good face on the matter, added, "That was a delicious meal. I always like French food."

Annie noted with dismay that he was serious.

The Creamers left early to tend Ian's outbreak of hives. "Don't go, Frank," Janine said. "Help Annie clean up."

After Frank displayed a dishwashing skill far beyond her own, Annie suggested adjourning to the sofa. They kissed and kissed and kissed. At the stroke of ten-thirty, Frank jumped up. "Another day of work."

"Let's continue our...um...conversation tomorrow," Annie suggested.

He arrived at five. After going out for a quick snack, they returned to become lovers. There was a small technical failure.

"You're just excited," Annie told him.

He left to go home and feed Max. "He's a wonderful cat. You'll have to meet him. But he really likes to eat."

"Like his master."

"Go to hell."

She expected never to see him again.

He called the next day. "I've been thinking over our technical problem, and I think I found a solution."

On Tuesday evening, the engineer proved himself correct. Both of them satisfied, he stayed on in bed. "I left food for Max," he said.

He had acne scars, a bald spot, and more body hair than most primates. She had bunions, knock knees, and enough belly to pass for pregnant. Yet they had an endless appetite for each other.

Wednesday passed in a blur of warm feelings and exhaustion. When Frank called, Annie suggested that they try sleeping the next time they got together. He considered sleeping a huge joke and wanted to see her that evening.

"Sorry, I have a meeting."

On Thursday, they bolted dinner and raced to bed.

He was leaving for Paris on the following Friday. She offered to drive him from his home to the airport.

"Get there early," he instructed.

When she arrived at three, he said, "Don't waste time. Get out of your clothes." They made love until an hour before flight time.

He told Annie to come to his house as soon as he returned from Paris. He gave the precise day and hour.

She feared that he might forget her and sent an aerogram to his hotel. When she received neither cable nor card, she began to believe that the affair was over. She had a sour, stale taste in her mouth, a familiar feeling of betrayal. He had seemed sincere, but then so had many others.

Upon his return, she thought to phone before leaving for his house. "Do you still want me to come?" she asked nervously.

"Of course!" he bellowed.

Frank had come back with black silk panties and less of himself. "I missed you so much I couldn't eat," he said. His eyes looked naked, like peeled grapes.

"In Paris, the world capital of good eating?"

"My niece said I was turning anorexia into a life-style."

They fell into bed.

Between bouts of lovemaking, they agreed on philosophy, politics, and the world order, everything but how to manage daily life. At home, Frank set the thermostat at sixty. Annie shivered in the cold. When night came, he piled his bed with a dozen blankets. "There's going to be a headline, Couple Crushed Under Weight of Blankets," Annie complained. Frank subscribed to the intermittent, although affectionate, school of slumber that involved periods of wakefulness ended by touching the bed partner. Annie rolled into a ball and fell into an aloof but deep sleep that could be interrupted only by a piercing alarm or human touch. Frank persisted in touching her whenever he woke.

"I really love you," he would say.

"I really want to sleep," she would growl.

She realized that the polite response should have been "I love you, too," but she wasn't sure what she felt. Her work load was so heavy that she hardly had time to think. She ricocheted from design class at the university almost an hour's drive away to clients at scattered points all over Greater Los Angeles to her drawing board. Making love with Frank seemed like just one more activity, although pleasanter than the others. He was very nice, she knew that—bright, funny, boyish, and totally without guile—but did she love him?

Her busy schedule prevented her seeing Frank every night.

"Sometimes I think you actually like to work," Frank said.

"Like my work? I adore it. Gee, there's some I would do even if they didn't pay me a dime."

"That's hard for me to understand. I work for a paycheck, not for fulfillment."

Annie considered the cabbage family a hardship of early childhood. Frank was immensely fond of cauliflower, not just the florets but also the stems, which he sliced and ate raw. After considerable teasing, Annie presented Frank with a notepad in the shape of a cauliflower, and extended her cooking repertoire to *chou-fleur Mornay* and *chou-fleur aux tomates fraîches*. Annie complained that Frank wore so many white shirts that she would fall prey to snow blindness. He sent away for stripes. Frank glanced at Annie's much-laundered jeans and asked, "Did you buy those new?" She gave them to charity.

After he introduced her to Max, they alternated the venue of their lovemaking between her place and his. His house betrayed the dust and decay that came with five years of widowerhood. His year-old refrigerator appeared virginal except for diet drinks and frozen dinners. Both went into the trash when she discovered he had high blood pressure. "These aren't good for you," she declared. He seemed to welcome the attention.

A day later, driving on the freeway, she realized that she must love him for she worried about his sodium intake and cared what would happen to him.

She told him she loved him.

He looked up from his cauliflower soufflé and beamed. "You've got to meet my niece and her husband. I know what we'll do. We'll all get together on my boat."

Thrilled that she would finally go out for a sail, Annie ran out to buy deck shoes. On the day of the sail, the wind came up, and the Coast Guard issued a small craft advisory. Although Frank and Annie drove to Alamitos Bay, the boat never left the slip.

His niece, Lisa, looked like a magazine cover, and Annie thought that she was out of her beauty league. Then the redhead played show-and-tell with her handbag, producing a hot-water bag, a pair of wire cutters, and a can of garbanzo beans. Lovely she was, but comfortably eccentric.

Annie worried that he had no bathrobe and bought him one.

Frank worried that she had no health insurance and one morning, as they were tangled in sheets, pointed out, "If you marry me, you'll have major medical."

Major medical? The veteran of perhaps a dozen proposals, she had never had one both so unromantic and so loving.

She was touched and confused. They had known each other less than three months. Their backgrounds met at no points whatever. His father had been a Lutheran pastor, hers was a Jewish butcher. She agreed with Frank on world problems, but they argued about blankets and lights and schedules.

The thirtieth or fortieth time Frank asked Annie to marry him, she said, "Max is very sweet, but I'm allergic to cats."

"I'll give him to my niece. Lisa has two of her own he can play with."

"But we hardly know each other. Let's try living together a couple of months."

"I don't want to be on trial," he insisted.

"How about vacationing abroad for a couple of weeks?" she countered.

"On our honeymoon," he said firmly.

Before they went anywhere, Annie arranged a much-postponed trip to New York. She would dredge up assignments, talk to her sales rep, visit what remained of her family, and laugh with old friends. Most of all, distance would allow her to think, to make a decision about Frank without consciously making a decision.

Even when Annie was a continent away, Frank wanted to stay in contact. "Call me collect," he said.

She talked until his phone bill went into triple digits.

They rarely left each other's thoughts or conversation. Even though the pair never sought opinions, they came anyway.

"She's an artist. You're an engineer. She'll make you change your life-style," argued Helen, Frank's sister.

"How can you consider a man with so little interest in your career?" asked Alan who had been selling Annie's work for years.

"Three months? You need to live together for a year," decided Susan of the five marriages.

"Are you trying to prove you can catch a second husband?" asked Winnie, a psychotherapist who had never married.

"What do you have to lose? Isn't California a community property state?" counseled Paula, whose business faced bankruptcy.

"Grab him. A plain girl like you, how many chances will you get?" advised her beautiful cousin Judy. "Incidentally, have you thought of buying mousse for your hair?"

Annie returned with smoother hair and her customary indecision.

The proposals continued. One evening, after she prepared a cauliflower curry, Frank displayed a sheaf of papers, smoothing them and saying, "See. This is what I can offer you."

The papers described his pension plan, and showed both the projected monthly payments and the lump sum that would come to him upon retirement. Frank ran his hand over the papers again as though the pages were pearls and rubies.

She glanced quickly through the pages without focusing on the numbers and then looked up at his earnest face. No one this good should have to offer anything at all, she thought. It was perhaps the most touching, poignant moment of her life.

Before she had time to formulate an answer, rain began to fall. Annie told Frank about her fear of rain. He held her closely, "You have me now, honey."

They went to bed.

It rained all that night and continued for days. At first, the thirsty ground sucked up the moisture, but as the rain continued to beat down, canyon rivulets turned into torrents, carrying soil, rocks, and trees in their wake. In the flatland, storm drains failed, and water rose, cresting the sidewalks and the lawns.

Annie fled low-lying Mar Vista for the higher ground of Santa Monica. Even north of Montana Avenue, the rising waters invaded the houses, forcing people to leave their sodden homes. They sought refuge in the basement bars, golden oases of light and warmth where the supply of pizza and hot dogs never ran out, and the kegs of beer and wine never became empty.

The bars took on a carnival atmosphere. Singles clustered in groups to sing and dance. Families gathered together, the old reliving tales of their youth and playing with the young. The children enjoyed their reprieve from school, and adults reveled in an unexpected holiday. It was a time of gladness, but Annie felt closed in and restless.

One day, during a break in the weather, Annie ventured into the street, shoes in hand, wading cautiously, the water lapping gently at her shins.

The streets were empty, and the air felt fresh for the smog had vanished. The cars had stopped floating and were now still. Under a gray sky, Annie kept moving to stay warm. She headed toward the ocean to look at the pier. It was empty and soaked, the snack stands closed and the carousel at rest. There was no sound but the surf. The world seemed empty and new.

Annie went down the stairs to the beach and saw that the storm had changed the shore. In place of the sand, there was an unbroken field of snowy white cauliflowers, stretching from the ocean walk to the sea. The cauliflowers were soft underfoot and miraculously dry, and although there was neither shelter nor people, she knew that she had found a safe haven.

When Annie awoke, she smiled at the sheer looniness of her dream. Flooding in Mar Vista? The area had fine storm drains. Basement bars in Santa Monica? There were few bars, and none in basements. Almost no one had a basement in Southern California, nor were people likely to rejoice when rain flooded their homes. But the cauliflower beach could only mean Frank.

She rose on her elbow and peered down at the big man. Frank lay on his side, mouth open, gray hair askew. Sensing her movement, he stirred and his eyes fluttered open. When he felt her breasts brush his back, he reached behind to draw her close.

As they lay together spoon fashion not saying a word, his body hairs prickling her skin, she felt protected and happy and totally loved. Without deliberation or conscious thought, she suddenly realized that she could not possibly imagine a future without him.

The first time I married

Karen Ethelsdattar

The first time I married
I took my husband's name for mine
& added Mrs.
I pulled it over my ears,
a woollen cap,
even when it scratched in warm weather.
I was his falcon, hooded.
I was his pigeon, banded.
I sank into his name like a feather bed
& neglected to rise in the morning.
I crept under his wing
like a fledgling
too small to spread its own feathers.

Now I add your name to mine,
proud & frightened.
This time I keep my own,
I surrender nothing.
Still this act
reminds me of captivity—
sweet & dangerous.
Forgive me when I grow fierce
& understand
when I seek wild mountain meadows.

Good-Bye Prince Charming

Claudia Van Gerven

she thought she was done with all that
had turned all the mirrors to the wall
given up meat, taken possession
of her gray hairs
but the story reasserts itself
persistent as the green joy
that rises in the lilac
winsome and upright as the sex of young boys
she hears it thumping through the night
trying to undo the latches
to break into her glass house
her windows loosening
like spring water

what should she do with the answering tattoo
gray hairs breaking loose from the snood
do they remember the fire dance
are they still red at the roots
how can she call his name
no longer being princess, no longer
being poor, what can he give her
but those same cold slippers dreaming
among the dust puffs behind the closet door
they would shatter in such tarantella
shards mining the threshing floor

where will she find her beauty now
not in the eyes of boys
clear as streams rushing over boulders

nor in the dark glass of downtown
office buildings where the King slinks
among his portfolios

it is easy enough to say
let her sing her own song
let her find her own way
among budding willows
on the creek bank, through
the predatory traffic of
the alleyways, will her words
rise up the glass walls
will the magpies peck them away

if she says I am beautiful
will lilac laugh
and laughing will she kiss
sleeping buds awake?

Old Friend Sends a Chain Letter

Therese Becker

"This prayer has been sent to you
for good luck. It has been around
the world nine times. The luck has
now been brought to you."

You open the envelope and people
begin to spill out on the kitchen table:
an arm, a leg, and poor Joe Elliott
who lost his four hundred thousand
all because he refused
to circulate the holy chain.
And worse, there's General Welch
who lost his life only six days after
he failed to pass on the prayer,
the chain letter sent to you by a friend,
and begun by a holy missionary
from South America
for those of us in need
of a salvation we could buy
at the post office.

The list continues like a voodoo obituary.
You pour a second cup of coffee,
gaze into its dark circles;
all the small lives link before you,
people cutting up rosaries
at night in their garage,

snipping necklaces off the necks of young girls
as they wait in line for a burger,
large dogs set free
with one clean snip of the wire cutters.

Their chain fetishes gone mad
attract them now into armies;
they begin to hack down
rows of chain link fences,
work their way toward your neighborhood,
your fence, your dog, your daughter.
You rise to latch the chain
on your front door
and the old ritual rises with you,
taking you back to the kitchen table
where you take out your pen,
reluctantly, and address the first envelope.

Woman

Lillian Morrison

After the thousandth insult
she wakes up to fury

having waited ten thousand years
like the people of India
under their yoke of acceptance
assaulted again and again
by barbarians.

She was Saint Sebastian
bleeding from arrows.
She has become Saint Joan

a determined guerrilla
in the centuries-old, undeclared
war against her.

The Choice

Lesléa Newman

You can carve out a life for yourself
just as your bones have been carved
from some larger bone
your flesh peeled from some larger flesh

Or you can lift the paring knife
from the kitchen drawer
and free the veins
that rise to meet the skin

There is no one
save the poems you might write

Bittersweet

Fran Portley

Dried acacia flowers share a crystal
vase with bittersweet berries
in my neat New Jersey living room.
Put the quilt back in the guest room,
friend, you know I'm too Victorian
to share your waterbed. Your music
and my poetry never made it together.
Still, I fell in love with something,
the steep walk down to your beach,
eucalyptus trees. Maybe talking
to you mornings in the cluttered
kitchen over a mug of reheated coffee.
The kiwifruit I buy in my supermarket
never taste as sweet as the ones
I picked with you in California.

Forbidden Lover

Susan Eisenberg

The forbidden lover beckons.

I refuse to follow until
nightfall cloaks
                    my heart-tracks
and all eyes are turned aside.

In daylight we pass each other coldly.
We wear dark glasses.
We speak in tongues and riddles,
our lovepoems coded in casual conversation or
passed under tables in large raised letters that
must be swallowed before we part.

Islanded
raised in dark barrooms and parking lots
nurtured on subterfuge our love grows
deformed. Plans orchestrated in
hushed phone calls mis-
communicate. We grow distrustful. We grow wary.
Voices of propriety
raise haughty heads in snickering chorus:
no blossoming   without daylight
without daylight   no blossom.

The Life I Didn't Live

Joanne Seltzer

I wish I never married
I wish I had fewer children
I wish I were a lesbian

I wish I ate less meat
less dairy
more *Umeboshi* plums

I wish I talked less on the telephone
celebrated fewer holidays
paid less for cosmetics
dropped more in the poor box

I wish I found less time
for shaving legs and underarms
more for visiting planetariums

I wish I lived in a hermit's hut
surrounded by edible berries
instead of lawn

I wish the loon called to me more often

Swamp

Kirsten Backstrom

There is a swamp behind Jillian Bremen's house. Sometimes, she imagines that she inhabits a fairy-tale castle, surrounded by a wilderness of lurking exotica. Sometimes, she takes a more practical approach and appreciates that she bought the twelve soggy acres for a song. The swamp breeds mosquitoes, but Jillian can tolerate minor aggravations. She has established herself here; she has made a commitment to this place. The house sprawls graciously on ground composed mostly of sandy landfill. The house and the land accommodate each other. But recently, they haven't really accommodated Jillian.

She designed the house while she was still a credulous college kid who believed she could create anything that she could conceive. She lived in a crummy studio apartment for nine years until she could afford to buy land and build. Now, she runs her own architectural firm, and her home is a project for her spare time. The house is her indulgence, her headache, her conception, her nightmare. It has sloping solar panels in the south wall, a spiral staircase at the core, a multi-leveled living area, and a practically separate basement apartment for her son.

She and Danny have lived here together for half of his life, but he has never taken much interest in the ongoing construction. Lately, he's preoccupied with his stereo, his girlfriend, and especially his car. The car is a green bug that squats with its greasy guts exposed in the carport under the house. Danny seems to see it as a puzzle to be solved rather than as a vehicle to be driven. Jillian worries about his tendency to putter ineffectually; she also recognizes the same tendency in herself. After all these years, the house is still under construction.

When she stands at the breakfast bar in the kitchen, she can look up through the bare lattice framework of the ceiling into the bathroom above. For years, she's been meaning to do something about the plumbing. Her ex-husband, George, insisted on installing the toilet, tub, and sink himself. She's not sure what he did wrong, but the pipes groan ominously whenever the taps are turned on, and the toilet has a tendency to overflow.

The rest of the house is in a state of perpetual transition and malfunction as well. She and Danny have grown accustomed to maneuvering around stacks of lumber and drywall. They put up with plaster dust on the furniture, in the food. They eat on any available surface, sit wherever there is room. The arrangement changes all the time. Interior walls have been torn down and rebuilt so often that it is like living in a maze.

Since the start of his senior year, Danny has been increasingly annoyed by this chaos. He retreats to his own domain. He is getting ready to leave home and feels no personal investment in the house. After he has gone, the choices and changes will be Jillian's to make, alone.

She is in the habit of working late nearly every night. On weekends, there's time for Danny, if he's around. During the week, she keeps herself too busy to think about how things will be different when he no longer lives here.

Jillian's half-hour daily meditation is her only real time to herself. If Danny and Stu and her job did not exist, she imagines that her whole life would seem like one endless meditation. The day's distractions would drift across her thoughts, but she would not attach herself to them. Invariably, she'd return to the gentle transitions of her own breath: inhale to exhale, moment to moment.

After work, she hurries through a gourmet microwave dinner. She scrubs off her makeup and changes into a sweatshirt and jeans. When she thinks about herself at all, she thinks, objectively, that she is in pretty good shape. She has always been thin, and her work burns the calories. Though she's almost six feet tall, she carries herself without slouching or apologizing for her height. She wears her long hair loose and casual. Jillian cultivates a kind of hectic, windblown professional appearance which elicits both respect and protection from those who work for her. She is known to be brisk and absentminded. She is known for her look of perpetual distraction.

No one at work would ever imagine Jillian meditating. It is something she does to reclaim herself from their expectations. She tries to forget all commitments: to her job, to her image, even to her house and son. Whenever possible, she meditates outside, despite the mosquitoes. The swamp is not comfortable or beautiful, but it is the one place where no one bids for her attention, where no one challenges her self-possession.

As she douses herself with mosquito repellent, the citrus astringent smell makes her think of how she used to hold Danny's wrist so gently while she splashed the stuff on his pudgy arm. If she got a drop in a raw scratch, he wouldn't wince at the sting but open his eyes wide instead with astonishment and indignation.

She wants to explain to him and to herself that parents and children can't help hurting each other. Thinking of Danny, Jillian wonders if she should postpone her meditation tonight and try to talk to him, even though he has made no effort at all to talk to her. When Danny doesn't want to be disturbed, he locks his door. Jillian has no such option, since there are few doors in her part of the house. Of course, she and Danny make a deal when Stu sleeps over. If Jillian asks for privacy, Danny smiles conspiratorially and stays downstairs. But when she's just meditating, he often interrupts. She doesn't quite feel justified telling him she needs this time to herself, so she meditates outside, where no one is likely to come looking.

Now, she decides not to knock on Danny's door. He probably wouldn't be able to hear her anyway. The floor is throbbing with his music. Jillian feels the pulse through the soles of her sneakers. The blunt thrum of the bass line prods at her. The noise makes her tense, although she doesn't really notice it any more than she notices the tarps that have covered the living room furniture for a month. The fireplace would be finished sooner if Danny would help, but Jillian is going to have to hire someone to do the masonry anyway. She stops to write herself a reminder on the pad by the telephone. The top sheet is scribbled over with the lush grotesque doodles that Danny draws while he's talking on the phone. The words *Dad* and *graduation* are engulfed almost completely in a welter of twisting vines and leering faces.

Like Jillian herself, Danny is a very private person. When his father called him suddenly after a five-year silence and offered to buy him a new car for a graduation present, Danny didn't tell his mother the details of the conversation. Jillian assumes that father and son will get together to shop for the car, and probably have dinner.

She wishes that she could warn Danny about George. She doesn't want him to be disappointed by his father again. She admits to herself that she is also worried on her own account. George might take advantage of this difficult and vulnerable time, to steal Danny's loyalty from her.

She knows that she can't press her son for answers. She can't criticize his father. She can't question his decision to use part of his college fund to travel around the country for six months. She can't ask him whether he approves of Stu, whether he feels crowded out of his home by the presence of a new man. She can't ask him if he's sleeping with Cheryl, if he's taking precautions. She can't be a mother for fear of compelling him toward his father, for fear of losing him. And yet she also knows that she is ready for him to go.

Tonight, Jillian really needs to meditate. She changes her clothes and finishes her dinner even more efficiently than usual. She decides not to pester her son with questions, not to distract herself from her essential time alone.

Outside, the dusk reverberates with the stuttering discourse of crickets and peepers. A bullfrog groans periodically. She holds her breath, listening. As the door bangs shut behind her, Danny's music vanishes. The mosquitoes flock to Jillian in a whining cloud, brushing her cheek and neck.

The house is surrounded by mounds of sand, an island of dry ground in the midst of the swamp. Danny used to be the only little boy in town with an acre of sandbox. When he started tunneling into the sandbanks, Jillian had to make him stop. He could have been buried alive. Sometimes it seems that his whole childhood, her whole parenthood, was a succession of narrowly averted accidents. This place was always dangerous, but something kept mother and son both safe.

The landscape changed over the years. Parts of the yard were leveled and cultivated. Enormous rolls of turf were spread like carpet around the front deck, and four truckloads of chipped bark were dumped along the flagstone paths between the house and the garden. If all goes according to plan, Jillian will have the backyard finished this year, and the stark sand will be replaced by a fragrant brown slope of bark all the way to the muddy shallows of the marsh.

Now, Jillian's sneakers fill with sand as she slides down the slope to the path. She doesn't stop to empty them. In fact, the cushions of sand feel soft under the arches of her feet. She was pacing a building site all day, exercising her best manners on the contractors who ignored everything she said. She could feel them winking at each other as she turned her back to roll up the blueprints. At least Jillian has the last word on their work. If they disregard her specifications, she can always make them tear the whole thing down and start over. She's never actually done this, but it helps to know she can.

The path into the swamp is spongy and ridged with roots. Everywhere, shallow water laps around the ankles of the trees. The swamp is a dark-green mirror with a dusting of pollen and pond scum. Sculptural crags of deadwood protrude at odd angles, reflected to create an eerie shadow-architecture of pillars which support no ceiling and stand upon no floor. The smell of vegetable decay is rank, warm, and sweet. Stagnant water leached through peat smells bitter as strong tea. And the soil itself has a loamy chocolate smell.

One year, Jillian and Danny dug chunks of the black mud from the bottom of the marsh, to fortify the garden. They waded knee-deep, stirring clouds of silt. The legs of their blue jeans looked green through the yellow water, and their feet kept sinking when they stood still. As they lifted their full shovels, much of the mud melted away. They mounded the rest onto a tarp and lugged it back to the house. It made the garden grow jungle lush, but they didn't repeat the project because of the leeches they found sucked on to the backs of their legs when they stripped off their wet jeans. Danny was only eleven, but he knew how to salt the leeches and scrape them loose. Jillian was proud of his coolness, his independence, but horrified at the same time.

Jillian's meditation spot is provided with a sturdy cedar bench. She sits, adjusting herself to settle her spine against the hard frame. She can feel all the angles of her own taut body and wishes that she were built of flexible amphibian cartilage instead of blunt bone. She takes off her sneakers and folds her legs into the lotus position. She takes three deep breaths, holding each as long as possible, releasing each as completely as possible. A mosquito settles on the side of her neck. She slaps it, feels distracted, draws three more breaths.

First, with her eyes closed, Jillian imagines herself saturated with dark water, absorbing tranquility through her skin the way that a hibernating frog breathes by osmosis in the mud at the bottom of a frozen pond. Then, with her eyes open, she takes in the whole surrounding swamp. She closes her eyes to disappear, she opens them to be aware, to be nowhere but here.

She always focuses on the mossy grotto of the embankment where a great drowned oak tumbled over years ago, its splayed roots ripped up from the ground. A curving earthwork of root and dirt still rises on the edge of the marsh, poised like an enormous clawed paw. The fallen tree bridges an expanse of still water. Moss has overgrown the embankment. An abandoned muskrat den between the roots yawns dark and empty.

As night permeates the marsh, the mosquitoes become more difficult to ignore. Jillian's skin feels itchy, clammy. She stares into the intricate wet network of twisted roots looming over her, and remembers the nightmare Danny had when they first moved here. He dreamed he was digging a tunnel into this embankment, scooping with his plastic beach pail. The hole was so deep that he had to extend his whole arm inside to scrape the bottom. And then the hole became the mouth of a snapping turtle. He was reaching down its throat while it choked and writhed.

Jillian blames George for Danny's nightmares. He was always teasing the boy. But the snapping turtle dream might have come from another source. The agent who sold Jillian the land boasted that he and a group of guys from the neighborhood had rid the swamp of vermin to make it more marketable. They marched in with hip boots and pitchforks to rout out, overturn, and skewer nine snapping turtles. The largest was a dinosaur the size of a Thanksgiving turkey; the smallest was no bigger than a soup bowl. Even the little ones could take your finger off, the agent claimed. He offered to do the job again if the turtles returned, but they never did. She would never have called him anyway. He told the whole story in front of Danny.

Jillian can't concentrate tonight. The distractions sweep her up and carry her along. She keeps imagining Danny's dream as she looks at the embankment eclipsed by spreading shadow. The roots appear to squirm, and the doorway of the old den gapes at her. She shifts her gaze to the swamp itself, to watch the water striders skittering over the skin of the water. Their feet make dents as though they were skating on gelatin. They don't weigh enough to break through.

A small frog lies in shallow water, quite close. Jillian didn't notice it before, and only just happens to notice it now. Its eyes protrude like floating bubbles. She can barely make out the suggestion of its shape, its legs trailing as it hangs suspended at the surface. She tries to concentrate on the frog. Although the darkness makes it difficult to see, she imagines it is watching her, with round amber eyes as intent as her own.

Memories bob up again, relentlessly. When Danny was a baby, Jillian would lower him into the bath and steady his wriggling body, while he flailed and frog-kicked. His plump belly balanced heavy in the palm of her hand as the water buoyed him up.

Jillian realizes that she is not meditating very well. She keeps forgetting to breathe. She unfolds her legs and finds that her foot has fallen asleep. She massages it for a moment, feeling as though she is warming a slippery animal in her hands. It is numb and rubbery. It is distinct from herself. It tingles, then stings, as she tugs on her sneakers. She leaves the laces loose, takes a few steps, and crouches by the edge of the swamp for a closer look at the small frog.

The frog is just out of reach. For some reason, she wants to see it swim away, to be sure that it is alive. She imagines that it would be safer overnight in deep water, rather than here near shore. She doesn't know why she can't leave it alone, but she picks up a waterlogged twig and reaches, just to touch it lightly, just to prompt.

The big frog comes out of nowhere. It lands with a splash between Jillian and the small frog. It actually jumps toward her, with a squealing croak like the creak of a clogged pipe under pressure. Jillian drops her stick and stumbles backward. She is reminded, absurdly, of her dread of overflowing toilets, that horrible embarrassment, primal panic, ridiculous guilt. She wants to explain, to escape. She's not really afraid of a bullfrog anymore than she's afraid of a toilet, but she is taken by surprise. She steps on her shoelace, trips, and staggers hard against the bench. Automatically, she scrambles around to put the bench between herself and the advancing frog.

It must have been hiding somewhere in a dark pocket of the mossy embankment. It is as fat as a guinea pig, leaping in clumsy lopes. Jillian knows that her reaction is irrational. The big frog couldn't really be defending the small frog against her. But there is no doubt that she is being challenged, threatened. The bullfrog squats, poised to leap again at any moment.

It is dark by now. She can't even see the small frog from here. The mosquitoes are fierce. Her meditation has not been a success. Ordinarily, she'd keep trying, but tonight she decides to do herself a favor and give it up. She considers stooping to tie her shoes, but the bullfrog makes another lunge.

Jillian turns and walks quickly up the path. The ends of her laces flap loose, ticking against leaves and roots. Her heels flop in and out. Somehow, her untied sneakers make her feel like a naughty child, hurrying home late.

She was not trying to hurt the little frog. She only wanted to be sure that it was all right. She only came here in the first place for some time to herself. This is her land, after all. She is no intruder. No one can chase her away. No one can blame her.

Ahead, the sloping south windows of the house gleam watery yellow between the black pillars of the trees. Jillian can't remember if she left the lights on herself. Maybe Danny has emerged from his basement to wait for her, to talk to her. She hopes he won't be able to see how foolish she feels.

The house looks angular and awkward, looming on the bare hill of landfill. Somehow, it doesn't seem to belong here. Jillian is a fine architect, but she has to admit that her own home is not quite right. Maybe the design was wrong all along. Maybe she should listen to Stu and sell the place. Maybe she should marry him, or move out on her own, now that Danny is old enough to be going away. Maybe she should do whatever she wants for a change. This seems to be the first time in her life that she has had a choice.

Actually, Jillian wants to go after that damn bullfrog with a pitchfork. She wants to flush the ugly thing down the toilet. She wants to fill the swamp with bark, just for spite.

Or maybe, instead, she wants to be an ugly, unreasonable frog herself, to swim down through murky water and hibernate in mud while the whole world freezes over.

At the back steps, she stoops to tie her shoes. She tugs the laces tight, as if she is tying up all the loose ends in her life. And she walks into her own house as though it is really hers.

Photo by Jude Keith

Amazing Grace

Susan Vreeland

My parents aren't waiting at the baggage claim so I walk out onto the street. Twenty minutes pass. I should have told them I'd take a cab; they've just turned eighty. I don't dare leave curbside to phone them, afraid they'll come just then. If they don't see me, they'll panic, think I missed the plane and am still in Los Angeles.

Eventually, I spot Mom's white bubble hairdo and Dad's side-to-side sway, his shuffling feet planted wide apart for each step, a walk perfected more than fifty years ago for stability on the rocking decks of oil tankers. He looks jaunty in his Greek wool sailor's cap, with Mom in mint-green polyester pantsuit, knocking shoulders with him as they walk, and all at once my resolve melts away.

"Sorry we're late," she says. "He wasn't in the right lane so we had to go way around." Her voice carries a perpetual irritation, a fact that she's always denied.

I hug them and rediscover how short they both are. I look down at Dad and feel again the shock at seeing the mauve-colored surgical scar peeking out his open shirt. "Happy fiftieth."

"Thanks for coming, Annie," he says.

On the way home Mom "helps him," as she calls it, telling him when it's safe to change lanes. I try to ignore it. "Don't forget. Turn on Oakdale this time, not Rupert," she says.

"She knows best," he says, then turns to me in the backseat. "Always."

"Watch where you're going, Stanley." She turns back toward me. "It's just that we never drive this far from home. Only to the grocery store and church."

"And senior center for Friday bridge," he adds. "Don't forget that."

Obviously an airport trip was too much for them. Mom looks at my face and her eyes narrow. I turn my attention to something out the window so she will too. "You look different," she says.

The wig—it's a fine effort, the same middle brown color, but a little too full. "It's the glasses," I say. "Did I have these frames when I was here last?"

"I don't know," she says. "It's been so long." She smiles her wistful, round-faced smile. For a moment I see her as I remember her from childhood—nourishing my brother Greg and me with tapioca and time. Trying to keep hothouse flowers alive in Philadelphia winters for Dad's homecomings from sea, there being nothing green and growing on board ship. Telling me that if you can do something for someone and you don't, you're never quite whole.

Dad's driving becomes more sure in our own neighborhood. I recognize streets where I played kickball, and houses of playmates. We turn onto Berkshire Street, the first address I ever memorized. Riding behind them, I feel I am again their child, holding the weight of an untold secret in my lap, a piece of news they will unwrap like a grotesquely empty present. The leaves carpeting the lawns on our block remind me of my childhood duty every autumn. Guilt for not always having done it lies like a dark pool in my chest.

"My God, the eugenia has grown so much you can barely see the house," I say. The hedge is wild and sprawly, over five feet high. "I remember when Greg used to jump it."

"Before it finally outgrew him," Mom says.

"It makes the house look kind of secretive hiding behind it," I say. Dad scowls slightly and makes an abrupt turn into the drive. The rear tire bounces over the curb. We lurch sideways but he pretends it didn't happen.

That evening Greg calls from New York. At the last minute he can't make it. Pressing business. I half expected that. His executive success excuses him.

She's gushy to him on the phone, but after she hangs up, she speaks bitterly against him for not phoning earlier so she wouldn't have told her friends he would be there.

"He probably couldn't help it," I say, by now a family refrain.

"He doesn't call as much as you do. Sometimes it's two weeks or more." In this way, she lets me know how often I've been expected to call. I haven't met the quota either.

We say good night and I walk down the hall to my girlhood bedroom, close the door, and look at the doorjamb. The secrecy lock they indulged me when I was twelve is still there. The latch is stuck, repainted a couple of times. With a nail file, I chip it loose. Ivory paint flakes off to show the salmon color I had in high school, the powder blue of elementary school. Maybe they'll never notice. I get the lock to work, take off the wig, and avoid the mirror above the dresser. I want to be in control of how and when I'll tell them.

Before we leave for the party the next evening I hear Mom's voice in their bedroom. "You're not going to wear those baggy pants. They make you look like an old man."

"Why, certainly not," Dad says. "What would you like me to wear? You tell me and I'll put it on." I wonder if Mom hears his sarcasm. She never appears to.

The living room of the neighbor's house is decorated in gold crepe paper with a Happy Golden Anniversary banner hanging over a dozen casseroles and Jell-O salads laid out on card tables. There are mostly people from church, a few from Dad's union.

"After fifty years, how many dinners have you cooked?" Mom's friend, Helen, asks.

The hostess gets out a calculator. "It comes to 18,250," she says.

"And every one was delicious, too."

Approving laughs at Dad's comment. Mom shakes her head. She can't accept a compliment.

The sheet cake has gold bells and Estelle and Stanley, In Love Forever written in script. Mom gets teary when she sees it. There's talk about the decades and the children's births, Greg's marriage, the two grandchildren. Helen asks her when each of us was born. "Greg was in '46, just after the war. September 20, a Friday at three o'clock in the afternoon. And Annie was March 6, 1949, a Sunday at eleven at night."

"Incorrect, Mrs. Burnside," Dad says. A smile streaks across his face but he does not look at her. "Greg was at eleven at night and Annie was at three in the afternoon." Everybody laughs. Mom looks confused, doesn't want to be wrong. I don't know who's right. Privately, I'm rooting for Dad, but know better than to take sides.

The collective present is a VCR and a membership at the Video Palace. The guests beam in pride. "Now you can smooch at the movies right in the comfort of your own living room," one man teases.

"And we will, too," Dad says on cue.

At home after the party I see Dad standing watch at the open kitchen door, saying his nightly good-bye to the sky, a personal ritual deeper than habit, left over from his days at sea. When he was home as I was growing up, he'd take me with him for this quiet observance on my way to "tucking in," the dark expanse releasing my childish news of the day. My heart turns over to see him still do it. I had forgotten.

I am convinced that when Mom is in repose, she rehearses the times she perceived herself to have failed, to have been found wanting, rearranging the circumstances to be more comfortable, whereas Dad, I'm just as certain, remembers moments when a pale star hung off the tip of a crescent moon or when the sky was a smear of purple above the open ocean.

I walk over and stand next to him, the cool air making me hug my arms. "It's still there, Dad. Your sky."

"Cloudy," he says. "No stars tonight. The night before you came I saw the Milky Way."

"Has it changed any in all the years?"

"No. Most things don't."

I cannot bear to dislodge his comfort in that thought, so I kiss him on the temple and go to bed.

In the morning Mom and I linger after breakfast, reading at the kitchen table. Dad fills the hummingbird feeder. He works methodically. "They're thirsty little creatures," he tells me. "And they depend on me. You look." He holds up the plastic tube with red sugar-water. "This will be nearly empty tonight." Carefully, he wipes up some red drips on the counter.

Mom reads again the wealth of greetings written on anniversary cards.

"Would you like another cup of coffee, Mrs. Burnside?" It's the name he uses in moments of mock gallantry or easy peace. He leans forward slightly at the waist, with the polish of a butler in slow motion. "To go with the cards?" She says yes and he takes a painfully long time to decide where the parts of the coffee maker go, even though he's done it every day for years. It's his job, just like taking out the trash. "Have you collected some trash for me, Mrs. Burnside?" he asks every afternoon.

He slides his feet across the kitchen linoleum. "Pick your feet up," she says. I wince. He doesn't hear her.

He pours the coffee and mutters, not a question, "What's the point of picking them up if they're going to come back down again."

I notice that the microwave I sent them last Christmas still has the instruction book and warranty sitting in it, even though it was the simplest one I could find. I go over its operation with Mom. She's distracted, wants to tell me news about the children and illnesses of each person at the party. I try not to listen, until I hear about someone taking prednisone. I go into my bedroom and zip mine into my suitcase.

Later I hook up the VCR to the television and try to explain to Dad how it functions. For the time being, it sits on the floor. Mom frets over not having the right furniture to accommodate it.

The paperboy comes to collect and Dad goes into the bedroom for his wallet. He's there a long time. Eventually Mom follows him. "Don't keep him waiting, Stanley."

"No, no, I wouldn't think of it."

"Well, what's the problem?" He mumbles something I can't hear. "You can't find your wallet? Again?" Her voice has the edge of a scalpel. "Isn't it here on your dresser?" I hear drawers opening. "If you put it in the same place every day, you'd always know where it is."

"Why certainly, you're absolutely right."

His voice is steady. I wonder if his wounds had formed scars so completely that he had no more feeling close to his heart.

"I'll go pay him." Mom bustles to the front door with her purse, pays the paperboy, and whispers to me, "Do you see what I have to contend with? He can't do anything anymore." She returns to the bedroom. "Did you find it?"

He mutters a no. I wish he had.

"You've got to take care of your things," she says. "I can't do everything. Where'd you put it last?"

He must not remember; that's why he doesn't say. I go into the bedroom to help them look—under the dresser, the bed, the chair.

"Maybe it slipped behind the dresser," he says. I step toward it quickly to pull it out. I don't want him doing it. The wallet isn't there.

"Is it still in the pants you wore last night?" Mom asks. We look in the pocket. Not there. We fan out through the house. I spot the wallet on the counter by the kitchen door.

He is baffled. "Isn't that something? How could it get there?" And he's embarrassed. In front of his wife of fifty years and his own daughter. I give Mom a quick look so she won't say anything more. We watch as he goes outside. I know that it is to be alone.

I avoid eye contact and retreat to the bathroom, where I splash water on my face and ache. The cool water is soothing and I bury my face in terry cloth.

Mom corners me when I come out. "A few weeks ago he turned left into the pharmacy right in front of an oncoming car and the driver swerved and yelled something awful to him. He moped around for days, but he did drive me to my hair appointment when it was time."

"How long has it been since you drove?"

Mom lowers her eyes, looks serious. "I know, I know. I'll practice around the neighborhood."

"Maybe while I'm here I should drive with you a little."

She shakes her head. "I'll do it."

Hours later the sound of Dad's harmonica croons through the hallway. Mom freezes, listens. A few notes in and we recognize "Amazing Grace." We tiptoe through the kitchen to hear better. Her eyes get watery. I tease her with a smile. "I can't help it," she says. "When he does those fluttery parts, it's just beautiful, but lonesome, too." As the music continues she intones the words, "That saved a wretch like me." Shyly she reaches for my hand. "It's the getting old," she says in defense of her tears, but the melody is haunting to me, too. I nod because I do not trust my voice.

The next day Mom and I look through the Sears home catalog to choose new drapes for the den, my gift to them. We settle on a silvery gray. "Don't you want to ask him?"

"No. He'll like this. I'll show him later." The conversation moves to where it left off the day before. "All he does is read both newspapers, watch CNN, and worry about the world," she says. "He falls asleep in his chair and he forgets to take his medicine."

"Ssh, Mom. He's right in there."

"He can't hear us." Her shoulders and chest heave in a great, tired sigh. "He puts too much salt on his food and it's not good for him. I try to cook fish. Dr. Morris said I should, but I hate to. It smells up the house and it's more expensive."

"You can afford it, Mom."

She shakes her head. "I try to take care of him, but everything's on my shoulders. When the water heater broke last spring I had to call the repairman—he couldn't do it, he never calls anyone—and I had to make the decision between a thirty-gallon and a forty-gallon tank."

I feel I've got to know everything, so I ask, "What else?"

"I make all the appointments. I figure out the medical insurance forms."

I know she's been saving all this up to tell me. "What else?"

"He forgets to feed the hummingbirds. I have to remind him. He used to do it like clockwork every morning."

"What else?"

"He says he's going to leave me."

She stares at the Sears catalog. Both of us are silent, in respect for the words just said. She shifts position in her chair.

"You don't believe him, do you?"

"He says he'll go to the Seaman's Home."

Below her pinched mouth, her chin quivers. All she's done for others, all the lunches packed, the laundry, all this seems to have melted away without due recompense and left her empty and confused. Lines tighten around her eyes, which plead for me to do something.

"I'm sorry, Mother. You shouldn't have anything to worry you." I take her hand in mine. "If I could do anything in the world so you wouldn't have any worries, I'd do it."

"I know." She pats my wrist. "Wait here." She grasps the armrests of her chair and pushes herself up and into the bedroom. In a minute she returns, her large-freckled hand in a fist surrounding something small. She says nothing, her lips pulled in tightly, but motions for me to hold out my hand. I do. She uncovers a satin ring box. I look up at her, aghast. She gives a vigorous nod. I open it and see the ruby ring Dad gave her on their silver anniversary.

"You should be wearing a nice ring," she says.

"No, Mom." I know she's making reference to my still-unmarried state.

She nods again, more firmly. "I've worn it twenty-five years. Time for it to be moving on." The lines in her face bow into a luminous smile and her eyes gleam. "Put it on."

I slide it on and feel the weight of its elegance. "It's lovely." I venture on shaky ground. "You didn't give each other gifts this time."

"No. Under the circumstances." She sighs. "Or maybe we're just tired." She pulls a handkerchief from her sleeve and blows her nose. "Is there anyone special you're seeing?" she asks, it finally dawning on her that she hasn't asked me anything of my own life—my friends, my job, my condo.

I shake my head. "But that's OK, Mom. I've been doing a lot of things I've always wanted to but used to put off. I go to plays whenever I want and I take a walk on the beach every day."

Her mouth registers approval. She looks at the ring. "Stanley was right. I figured it out. You were at three in the afternoon."

"Why don't you tell him?"

"He doesn't care. He's forgotten it."

Greg calls to see how the party went. I talk to him on the den phone after Mom hangs up from the living room. "They're old, Greg. You haven't been here. You don't know. You'd better start coming around more."

"I know. You're right."

"I can't be the only one they depend on anymore."

"I know," he says, impatient.

I lower my voice. "Greg, I can't talk now, but I'm going to have to call you. We have to talk. Seriously. They're going to need you, Greg."

"Sure, whenever." His breeziness is irritating.

"Do you remember them bickering when we were growing up? Did they hide it or what?"

"Come on, Annie. Don't tell me you never noticed it before. It's been going on forever."

"But it's worse. It's as though all these years of living without us made them careless about keeping it private."

"Look, just don't let it get to you. You can't do a thing about it."

"It's pretty pathetic, really. Two old people, still after fifty years trying to learn how to live with each other." I make him promise to call them more often.

That afternoon I hear the high whine of a motor. In the kitchen Mom and I look up at each other, wondering what it is.

Out the front window we see Dad step up onto a ladder and whack at the eugenia hedge with the electric clippers. He's so short it's a reach for him. Mom marches out the front door and I follow.

"Stanley, what do you think you're doing? You can't do this. Dr. Morris laid down the law."

He doesn't answer her, but takes another pass at the top of the hedge. The teeth of the blades grab at a tough branch and he staggers back, but hangs on, and it cuts through.

"Stanley. Stop it." She pounds on his thigh.

He wheels around above her on the ladder, the blades slicing the air two feet from her head. The motor rips through the neighborhood. They hold the pose for a threateningly long minute, the blades vibrating. His mouth is a straight line, his eyes narrow. He looks foreign to me, strangely tall and menacing. "Go back in the house, Estelle."

Mom's quick glance across the street checks the neighbors' windows. She is aware of the picture this gives. She backs away. With a quick flip of her hand she motions me to follow her; she's always thought proximity implies allegiance.

"This is ridiculous, Dad. You don't have to do this." He has turned back to the hedge and can't hear me above the grind of the motor. I retreat to the house.

Peering out the living room window, Mom says, "See what I have to contend with? See? He shouldn't be doing that. Dr. Morris told him to slow down."

"But when he does slow down, you complain he's not doing anything."

Mom glares at me, then begins to cry and her eyes plead. Like so many times before, I take her round soft form into my arms and bend over her. "He doesn't hold me anymore," she whispers, and in that moment I know that any added ounce of worry would catapult her over the edge.

"We'll get a gardener," I say. She shakes her head. "Why not?"

"He won't have it."

"The same way you won't have a housekeeper?"

"I can't sit there while someone else cleans my house."

"Then schedule it on Friday when you go to bridge." Another head shake. "Why not?"

"Not when I'm not here."

I walk into the kitchen to get the Yellow Pages. She pads behind me. I turn to the H's. She sulks. "He's not dressed warm enough either. He only has on that thin cotton jacket." She scours the sink as if it were alive with vermin, and runs the water full force. I see in her slightly puffy face a sad, worn love, wrenched by confusion.

We hear the motor roar wildly, the crash of metal hitting cement, the ladder falling against the sidewalk. Mom and I bump hips getting through the front door.

Dad is lying in a tangle of cord and ladder. Above his left eyebrow a gash is bleeding. His eyes are open but he is dazed and unfocused. I'm conscious of Mom screaming, "Do something. Do something."

I disconnect the hedge clippers. "Get a dish towel," I say. Mom moves as if fifty years had rolled back. I stanch the wound, which is more messy than deep, and we get him into the house. He refuses to go to the emergency room.

"I told you. I told you you shouldn't be doing that." Deftly, happy to be in charge, Mom cleans and wraps the wound and puts him to bed. He looks pathetic and angry. Against his protestations, Mom serves him dinner on a bed tray. We all eat in the bedroom. When she leaves to take the dishes away, he admits to me quietly that he "had a spell or something" on the ladder.

"Did you have heart pains?" I ask. He shoots me a glance, then looks away and shrugs. "Why won't you go to Dr. Morris?"

"I don't like him much anymore. All he does is run tests, and he doesn't tell me anything, and then I get a big bill, so what's the point?"

Better than he can guess, I understand, and let it go.

The week is over and I'm due back in California. Mom insists we leave for the airport two hours before my flight. "He might get lost," she says. I counter her, saying I'll take a cab, as much to show her how simple it is as to avoid an ordeal.

Part of me would like to stay to help them—to hire a housekeeper, a gardener, take Dad to Dr. Morris, give Mom driving lessons or hire a driver. But part of me is glad to escape into the world of competence and reason.

The cab comes, and we walk by the butchered eugenia hedge, some of it a foot shorter than the rest, most of it with wild branches growing askew above the mass. Better the hedge than each other, I think.

We hug. "I like your perm. Meant to tell you," Mom says. Then, "Get in, get in," afraid the meter is running already.

"Don't worry about us," Dad says, a square of gauze taped to his forehead.

As the cab nears the corner, I look out the back windshield. I had hoped I would see that it wasn't worth it, that all those years only brought bitterness, that I wouldn't miss much. Instead, I see them clawing to hold on, two tiny figures leaning against each other in front of the hedge.

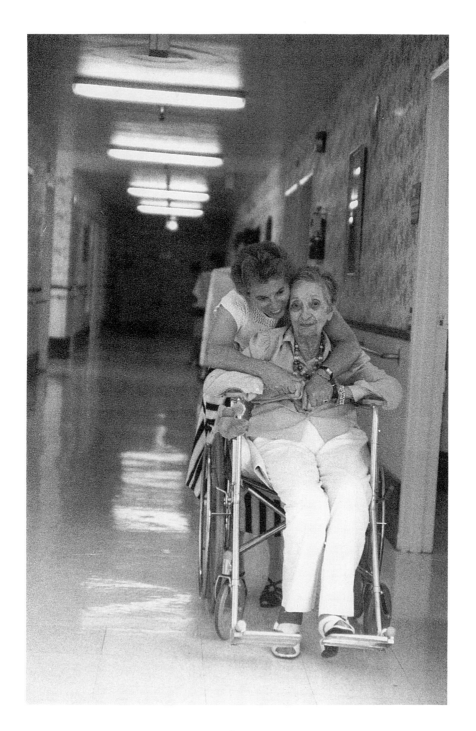

Photo by Lori Burkhalter-Lackey

Photo by Marianne Gontarz

If I Could Begin Again

Sue Saniel Elkind

grow
as a speck of dust would grow
then let me begin
by being a better daughter.

Let me begin by understanding
the silence of your life;
by showing you the sounds of
sight:
how a peach full in the sun
might be the sun,
how a flock of starlings
fanning the sky
is like one large wing,

by remembering Dad's gentleness
his quiet but deliberate way
of speaking, so easily read by you.
Let me begin with patience—
that I need not shout,
simply face you
when I speak.

Shopping Expedition

Elisavietta Ritchie

"Summer is a dead season," the motel owner says.

What tropic rampage of life around his pastel pillboxes: scarlet hibiscus and purple bougainvillea entwine with pale clematis, innocent honeysuckle and Virginia creeper mingle with poisonous pink oleander.

My mother's neighbor is waiting outside in his sapphire Lincoln Continental. I watch him from inside, here by the registration desk. He does not seem to notice me. Perhaps he feels it indiscreet to be observed leaving a motel with me. He was kind enough to come here for me. He is vain enough to comb his waxy silver hair for me.

My brother took over my mother's Volkswagen when he flew in this morning. He is also not afraid to sleep in her bed tonight. This afternoon he is meeting with her lawyers.

The motel owner is flipping the Yellow Pages for the closest coffin store. His first time to have to look up this item. Also mine.

Finally, among Fruits & Vegetables (Wholesale), and Fuel Ejection Systems, Fund-Raising Counselors, and Furs, we find numerous Funeral Directors.

I write down six addresses, thank him, walk out to the car. After the motel gloom, the sun is terribly bright, and I am warm in the black silk dress borrowed from my mother, or rather, her closet. Strangely, it fits.

My mother's neighbor gets out, shakes my hand solemnly, opens the other door for me. He squeezes my arm, as if to offer condolences, or something else.

We have talked long on my previous visits. Fortunately, now he is saying he does not know what to say. I show him my list of addresses.

"They are scattered all over the suburbs," he points out, "or in the seedier sections of town."

I think of certain foreign cities where one whole street, fragrant with pine shavings and incense, devotes itself to the craft, and funeral revelers gong full blast all across town so everyone knows and in some way shares in the celebration.

She would have shunned such exotic show, as well as funeral parlors.

Cold in the car, I roll down the window, welcome the heat which billows inside, licks the white leather seats with its stream.

"That doesn't help the air-conditioning," he murmurs, leaning toward me. He keeps squeezing my hand.

"That doesn't help your driving," I murmur back.

He continues to careen through the streets as if late for a wedding.

The first showroom stands among beauty parlors and package stores, used car dealers and billiard halls, in a neighborhood my mother would not have frequented. Nor would my mother's neighbor. He is busy unfastening my seat belt with more than condolent warmth.

Terribly cold in the showroom. The salesman, large in a dark shiny suit with a faded carnation in the lapel, extols the value of velvet linings.

"But my mother hates velvet. Besides, velvet's too hot for this climate."

"Then rayon? Or satin? Or best of all silk; see how nicely striped—"

Like Grandmama's love seat, I think.

"Feel here," he says, "how soft this padding is. And see here, these handles are hinged for ease of pallbearing."

I think how my brother and my mother's neighbor and her lawyer and maybe her dentist will all together give a jolly heave ho, even a *Yo, heave ho*. . . .

"And let's consider oak versus walnut—"

Or whatever wood lasts almost forever, and with age might improve.

"My mother insists on cremation. No point in sarcophagi at $4,995."

The salesman inhales. "For a dignified burial service—"

Distaste on his florid face. He doesn't want his coffins in the fire. He shows me the line in the catalog that guarantees imperviousness to groundwater.

No, as far as he knows, twenty years in the business, there are no reusable coffins.

My brother and I divided the chores: Should I have left this one to him?

The salesman steers us from coffin to coffin. Each appears more substantial, more plush than the last. Some have handles of brass.

I remember the Mother's Day card of padded satin trimmed with pink lace I sent her once, in part as a joke, but also. . . . It reached her in the midst of her myriad causes. She scribbled back on a plain pres-tamped post office card: *Why waste your money on kitsch?* I never sent her another.

In her sensible striped beige dress she is still lying cold back home until they come for her. My brother left the air-conditioning on High. That will also keep the flowers from wilting.

She would be annoyed at the stiff bouquets. "Sympathy gifts," she often said, "should go for worthier purposes. And lilies are so depressing, gladioli so rigid."

On the way home, we will surely pass a field or empty lot. I will gather her favorite daisies, as if for a bridal bouquet. I won't let them burn.

"Black is becoming to your fair skin," my mother's neighbor's whispers caress my hair. "But you're pale today beneath all those freckles. As soon as we've finished this business, I'll take you to lunch, feed you a juicy steak, or better, calves' liver, washed down with a good burgundy. You need extra protein and iron to carry you through this ordeal."

How my mother's neighbor sounds like my mother, except that she seldom served meat. It is *she* who lies terribly pale, back there, beneath her freckles of age.

"They'll fix her up nicely," the salesman is saying, "and a pink velvet lining will be most becoming. When the coffin rests open and you approach to kiss her, you'll note the fine workmanship under the lid."

Years since I've kissed my mother. When she was drinking, I couldn't even approach. Despite all her goodness. . . .

I insist that $4,999 is too much. So is $3,999. Even $2,999.

"This coffin is only $2,955." The salesman plumps up the plush. "The Basic Package with Options."

The $2,955 Package lies at the back of the showroom. Brass handles like door knockers. Let me in, let me in, in the dead of the night.

"I know it's a difficult choice," murmurs my mother's neighbor. His fingertips trickle over my forearm. "Shall I help you, honey, make up your mind? And after the funeral is over, and your brother leaves, I'll find an excuse to take you for a few days to the beach. . . . "

The salesman is distracted. His secretary, her coiffure glistening blonde helmet-stiff above her magenta blouse and black patterned slacks, needs him to sign several death certificates. He excuses himself, it'll just take a moment in his office.

Another door leads to a smaller showroom.

"Look over here," I tell my mother's neighbor, who is running his fingers over a gleaming Cadillac of a coffin near the front window. "Absolutely crammed with coffins back here!"

Plain pine in the corner, and what feels like plywood pasted over with wallpaper, or self-sticking shelf paper, to simulate walnut bordered with teak. A smaller coffin, gold foil embossed with dancing lilies, sized for a child.

"Prices are much better here!" I tell him. "And it's warmer, away from that air conditioner."

My mother's neighbor is wiping sweat from his neck with a large white handkerchief.

I finger the Dacron paddings. Orange blossoms and pink roses, forget-me-nots, and here's one printed with blue anchors. I think of the long-ago pajamas, patterned with little green trains, which my mother found at a church bazaar and gave to my brother for Christmas. He swore they were too large, then before he had grown into them, he passed them on to me unworn.

The salesman hurries in. He looks embarrassed. His long arms try to shepherd us back toward the main salesroom. At the threshold he positions himself, arms folded, between the boxes and us.

"These coffins are for Latinos." His voice is low surf.

"But my mother was Latin."

He looks with surprise at my blue eyes, death-white skin, telltale red hair. My mother's neighbor also looks astonished. Both perspire in the moist air which follows us from the back room.

"She was likewise Oriental and Black."

I point past them. "I'll take—that one over there in the corner, daisies printed on oilcloth. My mother will be happy in that, and yes, I know it is plywood."

Think how well it will burn, I muse, and write him his check. Some question as to whether he will accept it.

Back in the icy Lincoln Continental, my mother's neighbor sits very tall, and does not take my hand.

Hot Flash

Linda Keegan

On this hot April morning, spring is like August, seasons changing within seasons. A west breeze blows through the open bedroom window, cools the hot flash that sticks to Mildred's face. Her feather pillow, now twenty-six, as old as her daughter Carla, bursts when she fluffs it, feathers taking to the air as if they had a chance to be geese again.

Seeing years of comfort on the wing, she waves her arms like a madwoman, struggles, tries to catch them, as if she had control over something that had made up its own mind. Some stick to her sweaty face like sucklings, and she is almost grateful. Carefully, she pulls them from her face and lays them in a crystal box on the bureau.

At a time when life is weaning her from the ducts of choice, it is important to understand the reason she chooses to do this; to hold on; to control. Dry rot is a grave deterrent to usefulness, causing its victims to become brittle and crumble into powder. Today Mildred is fifty, wanting babies.

In her green car, Carla comes to visit, to talk, to bring potted flowers for the birthday. "You look young, Mother," she says. "The change is natural." They sit across from each other on the porch, Mildred staring at Carla's face lit lovely by the east sun and framed by the flow of her golden hair. All of spring radiates around Mildred's daughter, blooms as magnificently as Carla herself.

Mildred wells up at the sight, sees lineage, and like a sonogram with an artist's brush, she paints clear portraits of her unborn grandchildren. They are beautiful like Carla, high cheekbones and green eyes. They are holding Mildred's hand in the garden, picking daisies, planting marigolds. They are growing up, riding bikes, listening to stories on her lap, falling asleep with teddy bears on the old feather pillow.

"Mother, please," Carla says, "don't dream about children who don't exist. You'll just make yourself crazy."

Again Mildred glows, damp and blush like sweet crab in the sun after rain. She fans the flying heat, the telltale rose that rushes over her body like embarrassment, spreading dry truth like pregnant seeds, rising, then settling on her face.

"I remember how we struggled," Carla says, showing Mildred her map of life. No babies. Her choice. Maybe later. Maybe. After the comforts are paid for. She doubts it.

"Yes," Mildred answers, "I am listening to you."

Mildred is listening, she's not listening, her own body gone mad with the monthly screaming for blood. No babies, she thinks. Casual. Confident. Like No-Thank-You. Carla's happy to be alive. Yes. No. It has nothing to do with her decision. No, there are no names for what doesn't exist. The narcissus and white tulips, forced in clay pots, hang heavy with blossoms, will not bloom again.

Mildred stares toward the mountain, past Carla, beyond her to where petals skirt around the tiny feet of the magnolia like long snipped curls. She sees her in another time on the lawn, maybe ten, a towel wrapped around her thin shoulders, a bush eager to be a tree: the haircut, the first attempt to honor Carla's choice, uneven in places yet dream-perfect enough for a new young lady. Old memories run free as a mountain brook, ring clear as a songbird's trill.

The heat moves again like a busy chickadee, a sine wave in flight within her body, its peaks and its valleys working their way from the inside out, perching on her face.

"Carla, please," Mildred snaps, "I don't want any pills. My mother never took estrogen, and I won't take estrogen."

"She never had a choice," Carla says. "But you do."

Mildred wipes the sweat, the wet thin layer that spreads like years across her face. She fans again, refreshing her skin with the cool air, pulling the fragrance of the lilacs to her nose. But this shouldn't be; it's too early for lilacs.

"I've ordered central air," Carla says. Hot days like this so early in April, she worries about her mother in the summer. Mildred paints again, imagines the days ahead. She sees herself powder white confined to a cool box to escape the summer heat, cooped up like winter to escape the cold, a thermostat controlling her forever, providing her with all the comforts of life: the bird caught up in the talons of time.

"No," Mildred blurts. "I don't want the pills, and I want fresh air."

Carla stands up preparing to leave. "Well, you think about it," she says as she bends and hugs her mother good-bye. Mildred watches her go, so beautiful in green, so sure of time. She sees her again in another time with her new haircut, handing over her dolls to be held while she wobbled off on the bike they'd found at the dump and painted her favorite purple, the same as the hyacinths. Like then, they wave and smile, blow kisses to each other.

"Yes, Mother," Carla calls back, "I know I'm a comfort to you. Don't manipulate," she scolds. Mildred turns, wondering who will take care of Carla when the heat invades her body on some untimely day.

Back in the bedroom, Mildred recalls the pillow, the comfort, how it molded to her body in another time. On the bureau, the crystal box fills with sun, splashing pretty colors that look like flowers across the wall.

She picks up one of the feathers that had stuck to her earlier, cradles its scrawny body in her hand and strokes the curls on its head. She imagines she's in the garden picking daisies, planting marigolds. As her own body warms, she stares at the life in her hand, sees its eyes opening for the first time, hears it cry, wonders what she should name this little baby.

On Loving a Younger Man

Alice Friman

One day when I am ninety-one
you will look at me from the doorway, leaning
with your head tilted to one side
and I will wonder if you remember
how I too used to lean
and lay my hair down black and whispering on the
pillowcase fresh from the wash, or how
later I would turn
tucking my knees under yours
for the night's insensible hours.

        And if I haven't forgotten—my mind
gone blank as a sheet—I'll remind you then
of the old amazed look your face wore once
at how much your hands already knew,
and I will call you back
from the doorway
to adjust the sweater around my shoulders,
the robe in my lap, and take your hand, upturned
in mine, to show you how that line is still there:
the lifeline I once traced with my nail,
that day on the bench by the Ohio River, that first
time, when I—troubled—leaned my head on your shoulder,
sideways, the way I do now
and you will then.

Ripening

Joanne McCarthy

It is sad to grow old but nice to ripen
　　　　　　　　　—Brigitte Bardot

What she regretted was her skin, folding in
on itself like fabric, elasticity gone. Life-
juice that plumped her cheeks disappeared,
wrinkles cast their fine net across her
face, laugh-lined her mouth. Her eyes deepened.
The hairdresser warned her about the gray.
Leave it, she said, I want to see
what Nature will do. What Nature did
was remind her that ripeness
is all, that autumn is the richest
season, that preparing for snow means
building a shelter, that warmth within
withstands whatever winter howls without.

When the baby laughed, reached for her breast
even though milk had been gone for years,
she remembered sweet burdens of motherhood,
relinquished them gladly, her destiny
now another—grandmother, wise
woman, matriarch. The brain
holds what I am, she said, knowing then
that body was always hers. The heart
holds what I would be, the womb can rest.
She saw her life, and knew that it was good.

Photo by Marianne Gontarz

Eating Cantaloupe

Midge Farmer

I scrape the seeds
from a halved cantaloupe
pare off the thick
veined rind, cut and hold
a wet orange slice. I eat
standing over the sink.

Juice runs across the back
of my hand, drips from my wrist
forearm and chin
even though I quickly suck
and lap as I bite off
each chunk.

The brash color, variegated
texture and gush of juice
from the fruit give me purpose
for this day.

I am the fruit
seeds gone, wrinkly shell
peeled off to reveal
soft flesh covering muscle,
electric-bright mind
and life-juice still rampant
still far from being sucked
away.

The Woman with the Wild-Grown Hair

Nita Penfold

The Woman with the wild-grown hair
finds a metaphor for self-knowledge:

There was a younger time when the Woman
slathered bright paint on old furniture
puttying up the nail holes first
covering the flaws, the imperfections in the wood
praying for a time to do more than make do
knowing there would be a day when
she wouldn't need to cover everything up.

Comes that day she decides to strip
things down to their bare essentials
takes days to scrape layer after layer
of paint off the ancient church pew
oak barely visible through the milk-base
which won't come off no matter what
chemicals the Woman uses and she weeps
in frustration that she can
only go so far and no more.

Strawberries

Leslie Nyman

On the first day of summer Angie went strawberry picking. She had never gone alone before. It had always been Marty's impetus to drive out to the countryside. But this time the heat wave sent her to where cool berries fell like memories into her hand. Humid air, thick and sweet, stuck to her skin. The crease between her eyes relaxed while she searched along the runners for hidden fruit. The heat massaged knots of tension out of her hunched shoulders. She lingered in the sunbaked field until she had picked more than needed. On the drive home she rolled the car windows down to let the warm air rush in and tangle her graying hair.

Her neighbor, Edgar Jackson, was mowing the edge of her property when she turned into her driveway.

"Hey Edgar! Hey!" She ran up behind his tractor-mower.

He shifted the gears into neutral and removed his earphones. Angie could hear tinny music whining from the headset.

"Thought I'd give your lawn a quick going over. You don't want the weeds to get out of hand."

"Thanks, but would you mind leaving it?"

"What?" He turned the motor off. "What was that?"

"Thanks for the offer. It's just that I don't want it mowed. Not yet. That's all."

He surveyed the shaggy grass and sucked his teeth. Then he shrugged, started the motor again, and drove back toward his garage, careful to maintain his evenly mowed lines.

The stillness of the air after the turbulence created by the mower was a welcome calm to Angie. She turned on the radio hoping for Mozart and sat by the window. The smell of strawberries, the warm air soothing her bones, and music surrounded by quiet—June had these moments of perfection that could hardly be found at any other time of the year, especially the year that just passed.

Mechanical rumbling in the distance ruined the moment. "Someone's always got to mow at the most peaceful time of the day," she muttered.

Her neighbors, Jane and Fiona, banged on the kitchen door.

"Can we come in to visit, Ang? It's just us."

"Might as well, you're here. Have some fresh strawberries."

Fiona did not hide her eyes as she took in the two days of unwashed dishes. She fingered the toast crumbs dotting the place mat in front of her.

Jane spoke first as usual, "I'm getting too old for this heat. My Greg says that June is breaking all temperature records." She fanned herself with a magazine. "Is that why Tim isn't here?"

"What?" Angie could not hear across the kitchen table while Jane's husband mowed their lawn.

"We thought your son was coming home this summer to visit."

"I told him not to. It cost a lot of money to come down from Alaska for Marty's funeral. I'll go up for the holidays."

"We understand," she said quickly, "but your first summer alone . . ."

"We certainly understand," Fiona said with a sharp glare toward Jane.

They were all silent for a moment before Jane cleared her throat, "Oh, yeah, one other thing."

Angie wondered when they would get to the point of their visit. Sometimes it took longer than this.

"If you want one of our men to help with the yard work, like raking or mowing, just say so. Lawns can get pretty raggedy come summer."

"I appreciate that." Angie was inclined to say no more, but Jane perched on the edge of her chair. Angie carried the bowl of berry stems to the sink and, not looking at either woman, said, "I'm enjoying the wildflowers blooming out there, right now. I never noticed those little smooth yellow ones before." She turned around to her visitors, "Thank you, I'll keep that offer in mind."

The street was quiet when Angie and Marty were newlyweds. There was only one other house down the road, and the strawberry farm next door. Over the years this part of town developed into a neighborhood crowded with new houses and laughing children on bikes. Fiona and Edgar Jackson's colonial-style house sat squarely in the middle of the former strawberry patch. He spent every Sunday riding his mower up and down in perfect boring lines over a lawn of weedless grass.

Angie explored her yard in the late morning when she was least likely to meet a neighbor. Colorful flowers were sprouting everywhere. The smell of honeysuckle mingled with an unfamiliar, nose-twitching odor in the garden. She wondered if that was the smell of wild sage. Straggly weeds tickled her knees and up her shorts. From the expressions on her neighbors' faces she knew they were losing patience. Soon an explanation would be required, and Angie was trying to find one.

"Mr. Kelson. I'm glad the Extension Service could send you out on such short notice." She pumped his hand. "Iced tea?"

He had a shy smile that relaxed Angie. It reminded her of Marty's smile, especially the crow's-feet at the corners of his eyes.

"As you see, I've grown quite a garden here."

"Quite a garden, all right." He scratched his head.

The yard was losing its domesticated look, like Marty on vacation when he hadn't shaved for a week. Green shoots struggling between the edges of the concrete steps cracked the little cement back porch. Angie led Kevin through the yard on the flagstone slabs Marty had laid their second year in the house. The stones ended at the hand-built brick barbecue grill. Sunday afternoon cookouts had been a regular event. Since Marty's illness she hated seeing it out there like an unused piece of furniture. Thick-stemmed plants grew around its base. A houseplant ivy left outside and forgotten about, now overgrew its small clay pot and was weaving tendrils around the metal grate.

"You've really got a collection here." Kevin Kelson smiled, showing a mouthful of crooked teeth. "Look, mallow, a nice cluster of mallow. Milkweed and burdock, of course." He walked among the weeds with the familiarity with which she roamed the supermarket aisles.

"There's lots of your clover, gone a little crazy. This is the reason why so many people mow. All this clover in neighborhoods that used to be pasture."

"I hate mowing."

"So I see. I had an aunt who refused to mow any of her property. All kinds of little critters lived in her yard. My father used to say they were the only ones would visit her. My mother said crazy old Aunt Louise had gone to seed. Mom was in league with most of the family to force her to mow." He looked up to see Angie walking away. "Gee, I'm sorry. I didn't mean to suggest that you and Aunt Louise..."

"That's OK. I'm sure many people think I'm daffy. Only, I was hoping that someone in the plant business might understand and, I don't know, be appreciative. But it's not that important."

"No, you don't understand. I was about to tell you that I got interested in botany because of Aunt Louise. Without her I would never have known the natural world exists."

He stooped down beside a white flower, "Look here, you've got bladder campion right next to milk purslane."

"What are these yellow ones?"

"That's cinquefoil, rough cinquefoil. Looks a little like strawberry, don't you think?"

Angie paused by a cluster of purple flowers. "I thought I saw a ram's head lady's slipper here, somewhere. It's endangered, isn't it?" she asked without looking up. "I can't remember exactly where I saw it."

"I don't see any. It would be pretty unlikely to find one in an old pasture." He walked to another part of the yard, "Look, bird's-foot violet. Nice, very nice."

"But not endangered?"

"Sorry." Scanning the plants he asked, "Are you sure you saw a lady's slipper?"

Late the next afternoon Kevin visited again. At the front door

Angie threw a wiggly-fingered wave to Fiona, who was watching from her upstairs window.

"My nosy neighbors are dying of curiosity about you," she laughed.

"I guess I should have called first. But I thought of a way to help save your yard. It goes along with your original plan."

"My plan?"

"Endangered species. It's a good idea. Unfortunately, there really isn't anything endangered here."

Angie laughed, "You caught me at my ruse. It was just an idea. Pretty silly, I guess." She turned away.

"Not really." He lightly touched her shoulder, "Listen, maybe you could make a land donation to the Nature Society. They require complete mapping. Then, they do a site inspection."

"Why would they want someone's yard? I'm not donating my house, too, you know."

"I know, I know, but it is something to buy time. I could map it for you, if you like. What do you say?"

Angie chuckled aloud while looking over her yard. It was a tangle of colorful vines.

"Sure, map away," she laughed.

Kevin came every day, just before sunset. He carried a canvas bag filled with pamphlets about grasses and a large hardbound flower identification book. Angie sat on the steps watching him study the flowers and leaves. Sometimes he held one up for the light to outline the veins. For another he moved it into shade to better determine its true color. Once he shouted out to Angie, "Great, you have fragrant bedstraw," and laughed with delight. She laughed too. Another time he droned, "Lamb's-quarters—God, I hate that. It's everywhere."

The vegetation reached unexpected heights. The unpruned hedge in the front grew taller than Angie, and hid a hornet's nest. Angie walked the long way around the house to avoid it. What had once been lawn was now almost entirely overrun with blue asters, white Queen Anne's lace, and a variety of gangly green spires not yet named.

Five o'clock Sunday afternoon Angie was basking in the unusual silence. Suddenly, the wooden frame of the screen door rattled loosely against the jamb. Edgar Jackson stood in front of her, his smooth face bent into a scowl. She had been waiting all summer for this visit and was not nearly as nervous as she expected.

"It's become an eyesore, Angie. Surely you can see that." His military haircut and ironed trousers suggested someone who did not sweat. "I plan to cut it down for you."

"I would rather you didn't do that, Edgar."

"It's an embarrassment to the neighborhood."

"It's my property and I prefer it like this."

"Like what? It looks like—excuse my French—shit."

"It's natural. The extension agent says there are some unique and interesting flora in my yard."

"That young man? What the hell's he know?"

Angie pressed her lips tightly together.

"We've taken a vote in the neighborhood and I've been elected to tell you we are mowing it down." The stiffness dropped from his voice. "Angie, Marty would have wanted it mowed."

The screen door slammed and Angie heard the mower rev up.

"How the hell does he know what Marty would have wanted. He only spoke to him to ask for jumper cables or cigarettes," she mumbled to herself while dialing the police.

Edgar drove his large tractor-mower up to her front gate and parked there, waiting. The motor idled like a bulldog with asthma. Angie stood on the porch. The machine's reverberations throbbed through her body. Shaking her head slowly from side to side she mouthed the words, clearly, so there could be no mistake. "I will sue you for this." He hesitated. A police car screeched to a stop in front of the hornet's nest.

Edgar looked up, mouth open, eyes wide. "You called the police?" He let out the clutch and turned the tractor into her yard. The grass closest to the street went down quickly. Stalks and stems fell under the roaring motor. A flurry of seeds and petals churned in its wake.

"Stop him! Stop him!" Angie yelled, swinging her arms and pointing. "Stop him. He can't do that. He's not my husband."

The two policemen standing next to their car smiled at each other. One stepped aside to avoid an irate hornet.

Angie ran in front of the mower and stood there with crossed arms. She had no idea what to do if he did not stop. She hoped the police would see she was serious. Edgar advanced, slowly. He waved his hands to motion her out of the way. She stood her ground. The machine's noise grew deafening. She could see he had waxed the fenders and polished the grillwork. Little sparks came out from under the hood. Fat tires rolled over the delicate lacework of leaves. Cinquefoil, mouse-ear chickweed went down.

Edgar's eyes glared blue stone. His face tightened. He was at war. He saw nothing but a stubborn woman standing in the way of his job. He blinked; he saw the two policemen standing beside her. His lipless mouth curved into a smirk and he turned his mower away. Deliberately driving through the middle of her yard, he left a trail of crushed stems and deep tire treads. Angie watched a swarm of hornets follow him home.

"We can't protect you all the time, lady."

"He may do it when you're not home, or asleep."

"Is there anything I can do?"

"Why don't you mow it? It sure could use it."

"I like it like this. I don't want it mowed."

"Better get a lawyer."

Angie stayed home all day and awake through the night, watching to make sure that no one came to mow her yard. She wandered through her house, straightening up the kitchen counters, shaking out rugs at the back door, and enjoying the sweet scents from her flowers. "Why should I have to mow because everyone else does," she said aloud. "I'm tired of doing things to satisfy the neighbors. Marty never liked to mow."

"Maybe we should get sheep," Marty had suggested after coming in from the yard, grass shards stuck to his sweaty body. "They could keep it trim and I wouldn't have to waste my time."

"I really don't think the neighbors would look kindly on us for that. Don't mow it for a while; maybe they won't notice," Angie had suggested.

"The neighbors! We spend too much time caring about what the neighbors think."

"Well, in this world we live with other people, you know."

"Angie, you're always saying that. We live in this world for ourselves too. If you ask me, the problem with this world is too damn many people living too close to each other. Everyone wanting to do their own thing but most of them trying not to get noticed by the damn neighbors. It can't be done. We should have moved way out to the country when we had the chance, when we were younger."

"Maybe so, but sheep in the suburbs is not the way to reclaim our youth. Besides, they'd probably eat his strawberries next door."

"That would be just fine with me. At least someone could have them. He never picks them all. I think he actually prefers planting and weeding to harvesting and eating."

Angie smiled, remembering what a mystery that was to Marty. He loved to eat. He had gained all that weight his last year, and she wondered if she should have let him eat as much as he did.

Hungry, she leaned into the open refrigerator letting the cool escape onto her body. She missed Marty. She could hear herself yelling at him to close the fridge door. Tears fell. She took a yogurt and drifted back into the unlit living room. The streetlight from across the road threw a soft glow over her wild shrubbery. The buzz from the light played its one note song until dawn.

The second page of the "Living" section of the Sunday paper featured a picture of Angie standing chest-deep in her garden of wildflowers. She wished she had not let Kevin talk her into the interview. The story made her sound eccentric. It read as though she were on a tirade about reaping comfort and strength from the beauty of nature.

That afternoon several people drove by, slowing down to stare at her yard.

"Are these free?" A woman stepped out of her car.

"Pardon me?" Angie stood up.

"I'd like some of these purple ones." She reached down and tore up a bunch from the ground.

Jackson roared across the yard. Angie planted herself between the hedge and the driveway. "You'll have to roll right over me," she yelled.

"Get out of the way. This is enough. You have lost all sense of responsibility. You need help."

"What about you, ready to mow me down because you don't like my yard."

"It looks like hell and you know it. Just look around, lady, does anyone else's place look like this? What are you trying to prove anyway?" He dismounted and approached her. "Angie, get out of my way. I'm mowing this today whether you like it or not. If you want to live in the wild go to Alaska with your crazy son. But people in civilization got a right to live in a peaceful environment."

"I could not agree more."

The sun beat down on them. His face grew red and tight like a beach ball. Her face was covered with sweat. He opened his pinched mouth to speak, but closed it again. He stared into her eyes waiting for her to back down. When her only response was a cold stare he raised a hand to her shoulder.

"Don't touch me." She thrust his arm aside.

"Angie, move." He pushed her shoulder until she lost her balance.

Rebounding back to his side, she grabbed his arm and pulled him away from the mower.

He jerked his arm with a force that made her topple backward. Her ankle twisted in a groundhog hole. While she was looking down he leaned his arm across her chest and pushed her to the ground.

Jackson glared, his hands wound into fists, his face daring her to get up.

Angie met his eyes, unafraid. She saw him hesitate, but before she could move Jane and Fiona were tugging on her arm.

"Quick, Angie, come inside." They pulled her up. "He'll kill you for sure if you don't get out of his way."

Angie thrashed to free herself from their arms. As they dragged her up the porch steps her shoes were ripped off. Her ankles were skinned and bleeding.

"Don't!" Her wailing could not be heard above the insistent lawn mower making its quick runs over her front yard.

When it was quiet again and she was left alone, Angie pulled down all the window shades. The destruction made her sick to her stomach. In the cool, dark house she curled on the couch and tried to think about Marty. But the newspaper scattered at her feet distracted her. It lay open to her picture. She stared at it. It was as though she were looking at a stranger. She narrowed her eyes trying to bring it into focus, trying to see it differently. Finally, she noticed the smile. It radiated from the middle of the flowers. It forced her to sit up. The neighborhood was silent when she put up the shades. In the glow of the streetlight her yard appeared unruly and wild.

Monday morning Angie rented a Rototiller. The high-pitched motor echoed through the quiet street. The smell of gasoline filled her nostrils. After the machine had turned over the earth, she spent the rest of the day working down on her hands and knees. She did not wear garden gloves because she liked the feel of the cool, moist dirt in her palms. She liked the way it settled in the lines giving her hands the look of a stenciled leaf.

Late in the afternoon Kevin stood at the edge of the yard. "Oh, my God, Angie, what happened? Are you all right?" His shocked voice unnerved her.

"Yes, don't worry." But his agitation made her see again the broken stems and wilted flowers stacked in a pile at the side of the house. Working in the yard had made it easy not to think about what was lost, now changed.

"What have you done?" he laughed. "I can't believe this." He knelt next to her.

"Strawberries, front and backyard filled with strawberries. Next June it will be beautiful again."

Photo by Marianne Gontarz

Old Women's Choices

Ruth Harriet Jacobs

We keep our thermostats at fifty-nine
so we can give our children gifts
we really can't afford.
We buy bruised, overripe fruit
from the distressed produce
and donate to our churches.

We buy our own clothes at thrift shops
but select grandchildren's presents
from the nicest shop in town.
We eat the same boring dinner every day
because we won't cook for ourselves
but produce a feast for guests.
We never say we need help when we do
but do without, not wanting to burden
those whose burdens we carried.

Some of us break out of these patterns
realize we have rights and choices
to care for ourselves too
but it is hard to forget early teaching.
Even after all these years
we put ourselves last.

Dearest Margaret

Eleanor Byers

Yes, we've agreed, when we grow newly old
to live side by side on your farm in Vermont
where we can raise goats
the small brown kind, following close
and bleating of love.
We've said we want cats, all colors of cats
to play in the shade on hot summer days,
to purr by the stove when evenings are cold.
And, Margaret, remember our plan to grow plants
with long Latin names
and prizewinning Bibb lettuce
for good-tasting salads.
You'll make tabbouleh (you do it so well).
I'll roast a capon (with shallots and beans).
How well we will dine
drinking mint tea or watered white wine
followed by cheese and sweet almonds.
Indeed, we can travel
wherever we like
as long as we're home by noon
to pet the cats, feed the goats
water the prizewinning lettuce.
When winter snow falls
we will pull on tall boots and warm, woolly coats
and slosh down our paths to the tin mailbox
by the side of the road.

To the postman we'll offer our best apple tart
hot from the oven, with cream
in exchange for choice letters.
(We'll write them ourselves!)
Oh, Margaret, let's read *Ulysses*
(again) and this time, patient with age,
unravel the prose of James Joyce.

Photo by Marianne Gontarz

Shrinking Down

Janet Carncross Chandler

Thirty-five pounds and half an inch
so far, in this shrinking of my body.
Homes and bodies sometimes act in reverse.

First, my country home began to flap
loosely around me, like a scarecrow's jacket.
Next, the condominium apartment I bought

felt like too much trouble—why
did I need two bedrooms, two vanities?
So   three weeks ago today

I moved into a retirement community.
All the old-timers welcomed me,
enumerated the years they've been here—

five, ten, even twelve. I watched some of them
move easily between the life outside
and the more relaxed world

of bingo, pinochle, and pool fitted
between breakfast, lunch, and dinner.
My twelfth-floor one-bedroom apartment

feels almost like home, a soft robe
of sunny yellow I can slip on when it feels
chilly outside. The thing I value most

is that tiny slot on my door, showing red
when I'm home and safe inside, clear
when out for the day. It lets the floor rep

know I'm still alive night and morning.
Strong bathroom fixtures prevent my falling.
And should I be attacked by demons

who specialize in old people
(like me) a yank on one of two pulls will bring
help on the run. *This* place seems just my size.

Keepsakes

Elaine Rothman

Someone's calling my name. "Amelia, Amelia, wake up!"

I don't recognize the voice, so I won't open my eyes. She's shouting as if I'm deaf. They all talk very loudly around here as if everyone is hard of hearing, and only some people are. They don't realize how rude they sound. Besides, if I don't know this person, she has no right to call me by my first name.

The sun is warm on my face. It sends silver shafts through my eyelashes. Golden specks dance at the end of every shaft. I hear a radio playing somewhere, and the clack of shoes along the tiles of the hallway. That's another thing they do a lot, walk fast and clump their feet. There's no thought for someone who might be resting.

She's still shouting, something about bringing me my breakfast, and have I forgotten this is bath day. It must be quite an event for her, a bath day. She's going on about time slots, and keeping to a schedule, and how I mustn't make her late.

Now she's calling me Mrs. Cochrane, and offering to help prop me up against the pillows and wash my face with a warm cloth. That's much better. I'll look her over and decide whether she gets a smile or not.

I don't usually care very much for any of the strangers they send to replace Margie. This one looks like a stick of taffy that's been pulled too long, stiff and stale. Margie's all square and deep brown like a chunk of chocolate fudge. She laughs when I tell her that, and says I'm always thinking of candy, just like a child. She told me she'd try to get here by noon, after her little boy's Christmas pageant at school. He's going to play Joseph, a beautiful brown-skinned Joseph.

Just as I thought, breakfast on plastic dishes, artificial eggs, and muffins from a mix. Decaffeinated tea in a paper cup. I ask this new one if she's real, but she doesn't have much fun in her. Real enough, and rushed, she answers. If I don't eat very much of my breakfast, that's all right with her, so long as I take my medication. See, she points to the word *medication* starred right there on her printed instructions. I notice that it ranks right alongside of *bath,* another starred item.

Her name is Frieda, she tells me through thin lips. Fussy Frieda. Says I get a yellow pill, with an orange one to follow. She must think there's no point in calling them by their correct names. Makes it easier all around.

Margie always closes the door softly behind her and whispers, "Amelia, breakfast time, honey." We munch cinnamon toast from real china plates, and sip fresh strong coffee. She doesn't have time to get breakfast for herself at home, so she has a bite with me each morning.

Frieda is pawing through my things, getting bath articles ready. We argue a little bit. Will it be a wheelchair or a walker this morning? I don't want either, thank you. I can use the handrail in the hallway. My strength doesn't usually run out until later in the day. She pretends to admire my red bathrobe.

I'm wearing red so Martin will see me flash like a flame through the woods. My fingers skim the tops of the bayberry bushes. My sandals skid along the slippery hill of pine needles. I must be on time or we will miss the tide. He promised to let me take the tiller once we are safely out in the bay. I can taste the salt spray on my tongue and feel it sting my cheeks.

Frieda sees me tuck the last packet of bath salts into the pocket of my robe and starts another ruckus. The water in the tub won't be very deep, and she's certainly not going to run it hot enough for bath salts to dissolve. There's a long list of residents waiting for their baths today. She'll show me their names posted on the door.

Margie gave me two dozen packets of those salts, all smelling of the spicy woods. She knows the stunted sand cedar. My trees are the tall spruce and balsam. We decided that it was the very same sea that washed both shores where we were growing up.

I hold on to the fragrant evergreen square in my left pocket. I need my right hand to grasp the handrail. We pass an open door where a very frail person is being fed the same stuff that lies untouched on my breakfast tray. The pleasant child feeding her is wearing a pink pinafore.

I once wore a pinafore like that. It had deep patch pockets to hold my favorite lunch, a slice of cheddar cheese, an apple, and a chocolate bar. A nibble of each, one after the other, until they're all gone. The trick is to finish with a single bite of apple, cheese, and chocolate, nothing left over. Wipe your hands on the pinafore when you're through.

I'm moving too slowly for Fussy Frieda. She offers me the wheel-chair again. It's true that the walk to the bathing room gets longer every week, but she'll have to be patient. There's no point in working in a place like this unless you're patient.

When Margie gave me the bath salts for my birthday she said she knew I'd especially appreciate the box they came in. It's gray-green with golden curlicues in a raised pattern on every inch of it, and a hiding place inside. It reminded her of the hiding place I told her about, the one that Martin and I used for years.

There was a crevice in the stone wall where steps cut into the rocky ledge slanted down to the sea. I scraped the golden lichen off several stones so no one would guess that one particular smooth stone could be pulled away. I lined the bottom of the hollow with club moss to make a soft spot for the gifts we exchanged. He left me plaid taffeta ribbons for my braids. I left him a rare yellow violet that I found in the woods.

I made a bet with myself that Frieda would show me the list of people scheduled for their baths the moment we got to the door of the bathing room. I assured her that they all know how much I love a leisurely hot soak, and wouldn't mind waiting their turns.

As punishment for my fib, I made myself look into the big mirror behind the nurses' station, something I usually avoid doing. In the mirror I see a little lady hunched like a question mark in her vivid red robe. Wisps of white hair sprout from her pink scalp. Her bright eyes peer at me from between her shoulders. They are the only thing about her that I recognize, the eyes of the supple, silly girl Martin Cochrane married.

I must have worn Frieda down. She filled the tub almost to the rim with water that the bath salts instantly turned crystal green. I close my eyes so I won't have to see her perched on a stool, looking at her watch.

My toes are luminous shells in the pool above the waterfall. I can barely see them over the hill of my belly. Everything floats in the clear sweet water. The striped wool skirt of my bathing suit billows around my hips. My brown hair streams behind me, pulling gently at my temples.

They say it is a dangerous place, so close to the waterfall. The rubber cap that I am supposed to wear whenever I swim hangs on a bayberry branch. Martin knows I come here whenever I can, but he won't tell anybody. He trusts me to know my own limits. That's what counts, Amelia, he always says.

I needed a lot of help getting out of the tub and toweling myself dry. Even Frieda saw how very weak the hot water had made me. She rang for a wheelchair and muttered about having to take my blood pressure as soon as she could get me back to my room.

I am much too tired to put up any fuss. Frieda hovers over my bed looking stern. She nags about the folly of trying to do too much at my age. Then she sits down to read my chart.

I learned to read when I was very small and Martin would leave me messages in our hiding place within the wall. DEAR AMELIA, he would print in big letters, and use easy words to tell me important things. I had to get it right or I would miss the tide for our sail, or the woodcocks whirring their crazy dance in the woods. Before I could spell out many words on my own I would reply with crayoned pictures that said what I needed to tell him.

I feel so tuckered out, I tell Frieda truthfully, that all I want to do is sleep. And if I'm still asleep when Margie gets back, please let her know that I won't be needing any more bath salts, but I do want her to have the box they came in.

She must think I'm raving because she looks at me suspiciously before she draws the blinds and darkens the room. She lets me know she has many other residents to take care of, but that she'll be back when it's time for my medication.

With one foot out the door Frieda shoots an accusing salvo across the bed. "Those yellow and orange pills will be the saving of you, Mrs. Cochrane. They might keep you going forever."

Margie and I have long discussions about what keeps people going. We both know it's a combination of God's will and good memories. That's why we tell each other stories about growing up by the seaside. She says it's a real pity that she and I and her little boy have ended up landlocked. What kind of good memories will he have, she worries.

My dearest recollections all have to do with Martin. I can recall every single surprise we ever left for one another. There were all sorts of love tokens, like the spiral of a purple-tinged whelk, a tiny spring of sea lavender, or a white gull feather.

Of course, once I grew up, there was the large lustrous pearl he would set into my betrothal ring. People could not understand why I would want to marry someone so much older than myself, but we knew it was the right thing for us. We were like two leaves overlapping, all veiny and insubstantial at either end where we lived our lives apart, but bright green and solid where we could share our time.

There was one surprise that did not please Martin at all. It was a spotted newt I left for him one morning. Even though I had punched air holes in the lid of the jar, he was annoyed with me. "Never keep a living thing captive, even for a short time, Amelia," he said. So I stopped collecting fireflies as well.

When Margie gets here around noontime I hope Frieda remembers to give her the bath salts box. Margie will run her fingers over the raised golden curlicues, slide the box open, and lift the paper flap. In the recess she will find the many pills I have saved like bright coins in a treasure chest. It is not a surprise she will like one bit, but we have always understood one another. She will look down at my bed.

"Poor lamb," I can hear her say. "She's really gone for good. I wish I'd been here sooner for her. She looks like she left easy, though."

Very soon I will be standing naked behind the waterfall. I will lift my face to the misty spray and watch the droplets sparkle on my sunbaked arms. My hair will lie in damp curls upon my shoulders. Martin knows where to find me. He will reach for my hand and help me climb the slippery smooth rocks. Together we will float in the quiet pool above the falls.

Counterpoint

Lynn Kozma

Insignificant
as a beached shell
I feel
the indifferent succession
of days
monotonous as ocean waves.

Bleaching with age
I have lost the rage
at my own
unavoidable demise.
But the mind still conjures
eclectic shapes,
the life of things
not seen.
Words dance across the screen
in perfect conjugation—
messengers of a kind.

Death, I know your winter face.
We have met in random places—
legendary landscapes,
halls of sorrow;

I shall wear RED
tomorrow!

Salamanders

Randeane Tetu

"I would not change one stitch, Margaret. Not one stitch in the fabric of my life." The quilt was velvet this time and brocade, and Emma poked the needle into the square she was working with featherstitch.

Wesley had put the bag of charcoal for the barbecue into a chair on the lawn, and when Margaret looked up, she thought it was a person and drew back a little and opened her mouth to say whatever it was she would say as soon as she identified the person and thought what words would be appropriate.

She looked quickly at her own stitching so Emma wouldn't see the mistake she'd made.

Wesley had the orange lawn tractor out now and had taken it across the driveway to mow around the daylilies. Noise and scraps of dry grass made a fog around him. Margaret remembered, in a shift of breeze the day brought, the smell of the sunshine on the dirt between the grasses while she stood, as a child, looking from the garden to the barn where the thin cool line of shadow lay against the stones.

"I wouldn't either," she said.

When Wesley finished mowing, he would take off his T-shirt and use it to wipe his chest and his chin. Chips of grass and dry dust would settle down onto the lawn tractor, and he would go inside and drink water.

She could see clearly the tops of trees and said again, "I wouldn't either," though next Wesley would come out and say, "Well, Margaret, it's a hot one," and swat the T-shirt over his shoulder to scratch his back, a thing she couldn't stand.

Next to the porch, honeysuckle grew on vines, its white and vanilla flowers strokes against the green. Burned-out flowers of the mountain laurel stuck to the laurel leaves. Emma held the thread taut from the square on her lap and reached into her sewing box, but she didn't take out the scissors.

"Now, you see that?" She held the thread and leaned closer to Margaret.

Wesley came to the driveway, and spouts of grass dug up the air, and noise pounded through it, and then the tractor turned away and grass fell down, and Margaret leaned to see. "What is it?"

"Ticket for an opera we never went to. Just before Harold died. And he said go to it. Take someone. But I didn't go. I didn't want to."

"What on earth do you keep the ticket for? In your sewing basket? Doesn't it remind you?"

"Reminds me, yes. Every time I see it. Keep my wedding flowers, too, and programs for the concerts, dresses that I've worn for special things." Emma still held the thread.

"Well, what on earth do you keep it for?"

"I keep it because later I think I'll want to look through and remember."

"Do you ever?"

"Well, I haven't yet. But I may want to. You never know."

"Now, see, it's the things I don't keep that I remember." Margaret leaned across with her scissors and cut the end of Emma's thread. "Like the card for Rubyfruit. I could have kept it, but I didn't, and I can picture that card today. Bright pink."

"And better, probably, than it was?"

"Better? How can a card be better?" Margaret said.

"Well, with all the edges rounded and smoothed over time, glossied and made perfect."

"Oh, I don't know. Do you still keep things now? I mean since he died? Things you want to remember?"

"I'm doing everything wrong now. Not eating breakfast and staying up late to read, and I don't have any concerts, and now it seems all lies. All, all lies and very much the truth."

"There must be something that you'd change though. Some little thing if you could?" Margaret was looking at Wesley on the tractor with the small island of grass ends and dust floating him above the lawn, and she was counting the rows he had left to come to the edge of the daylilies. She reached for a cracker and a sip of tea.

"Well," Emma said, "Laura and Grandma Ruth used to—don't you remember?—beat the rugs over the clothesline? Put them over and whack them hard...the one with the roses on it. And one time they were doing that, and Grandma wanted me to help. But I was doing something else, and I didn't want to help them. But Grandma was ready to get all excited so I told her 'put a lid on it.' And she did, and I hurt her feelings that way."

"Well, we all hurt someone's feelings. There was the time when Wesley and I first married that I was going on about something and nagging a little I guess. So wouldn't you know, he turned to me and said, 'Margaret, just drop dead.' And so I did. Hid, standing up in the closet, and he looked for me—oh, for a long time, and then he finally opened the door, and didn't I just drop out of that closet into his arms. Like to have scared him to death."

"Margaret, you did not do that."

"Oh, yes, I did. And the time that I first met Wesley, and my mother said don't mention. . . . The first time I met him I must have hurt his feelings awfully. My mother said to me, 'Whatever you say, don't mention his family. He's visiting here with his aunt because his parents just died in a crash.' And wouldn't you know, after we'd talked with him a while, there I was saying, without even thinking, saying, and not knowing that I was doing it, 'Next weekend is Mother's Day,' and what we were going to do. Still not even thinking of it until afterward Mama said, 'I couldn't believe you said that. If I'd been any closer I would have poked you hard with an elbow.' "

"Oh, no. What on earth did you do?"

"And then remembering. I near to died. I near to died, I tell you. And when I remembered how still he got when I said that and how he looked past us at the laurel bushes, why I near to died again of morti-fied shame and cried with it, I remember, two days, and then I began to feel—I had to do something—I began to feel he liked it. The chance to be dramatic. And that it made him special. He was special. To have to live with that."

"Well," Emma said, "we all have things we want to squeeze our eyes shut about. We are bound to. Don't they gang up on you sometimes—the mistakes you've made, so you want to crawl in a hole and cover yourself up? But you can't go back and make them right so after a while you just keep going, smoothing out the edges the best that you can."

"And then I kind of wonder," Margaret said, "if I didn't have to make that mistake. It really was a big thing to me at the time because I liked him. We had just met and all, but I could tell already I liked him.

"And I wondered, if I hadn't made that mistake and instead had been too careful of him, you know and not mentioned, like everybody else was not mentioning, why, if he'd have noticed me at all. I mean, what if he noticed me because of that stupid thoughtless thing I did, and because he could be dramatic, and it could hit me later, and he could forgive me?"

"I don't know about that," Emma said and took a drink of tea. "But there sure are things I never forgave Harold. Never. Even now. He took us all to family camp one year. And before that we were pretty close. All of us. In a family. He shouldn't have done that, though, taken us to camp so I learned they could do by themselves without me and I could do by myself, too."

Margaret held up a cracker, could see light through it, how it lightened at the prick marks and tightened at the wheat bits. Wesley was behind it.

"I wonder," Margaret said. "I've wondered for a long time if that was my mistake. Or if really the mistake was that I was sorry I had hurt him. And so I fell in love. To make up for it." When she moved the cracker, Wesley was behind it, and she pulled her fingers back so as not to touch him.

Wesley made a wide arc where the corner was too tight, and the lawn mower shot exploding bits of grass around him. Shatters of grass shot out like sparks, and Wesley turned the tractor.

"Yes," Margaret said. "Emma, there is one thing. There's something I would change." She threaded her needle. "When we were kids. Once we went to visit someone. The whole family went. She was called Jeannette, I remember, and when we got to her house, we walked to her neighbors' in the evening. Everything was dark and green and moist, the way it is on a summer evening near a stream. There was a stream there and wet stones."

The sound of the mower crossed the grass, and she counted the number of rows left.

"We sat outside, and the grown-ups talked, and I stood up behind the woman we were visiting and stroked her hair, brushed her hair with my fingers, and my mother said, 'Stop,' but the woman told me it was all right. Her hair was long and brown with gray hairs in it and later, when I asked my mother wasn't it pretty, she said no. But then she grew her own hair long and wore it long the rest of her life. You remember Mother's hair. Was long all down her back when she unrolled it."

"Oh," Emma said. "Your mother had wonderful hair. I always said she did." She looked at Margaret to see what it was she meant.

"I'm coming to the part I mean. I didn't come to it yet. On the walk home, well, back to Jeannette's house, we went past the stream again, but it was more like nightfall, and, down at the base of a tree there was a salamander. Jeannette saw it first—orange-coral colored, small, as if sticking to the wood, a brush stroke on the trunk of the tree—and I reached to touch it to see if it was real.

"Jeannette said, 'No, don't touch it,' but I already had. She said, 'His skin has to stay wet. If you touch him it will make it dry—just like burning him.'"

"Oh, I never heard that."

"Did you ever see a salamander?"

"No."

"That's why you never heard it. If you'd seen one, you'd know it would be true. And I wanted to not have touched it." Margaret looked up and thought it was a person coming up the lawn where the barbecue charcoal was in the chair, and then she saw it wasn't.

Wesley made the last turn by the daylilies.

"So," Margaret said, "what I said about Wesley, about maybe it was a different mistake than the one I thought I'd made? Well, let's just leave it, shall we? As if I hadn't thought it?"

"What about the salamander?" Emma said. "What happened to it?"

"Oh, I don't know about that. It sped around the tree and by then I knew it was real."

Advice to Beginners

Ellen Kort

Begin. Keep on beginning. Nibble on everything.
Take a hike. Teach yourself to whistle. Lie.
The older you get the more they'll want your stories.
Make them up. Talk to stones. Short-out electric
fences. Swim with the sea turtle into the moon. Learn
how to die. Eat moonshine pie. Drink wild geranium
tea. Run naked in the rain. Everything that happens
will happen and none of us will be safe from it.
Pull up anchors. Sit close to the god of night.
Lie still in a stream and breathe water. Climb to the top
of the highest tree until you come to the branch
where the blue heron sleeps. Eat poems for breakfast.
Wear them on your forehead. Lick the mountain's
bare shoulder. Measure the color of days
around your mother's death. Put your hands
over your face and listen to what they tell you.

Contributors

DORI APPEL lives in Ashland, Oregon, where she is co-artistic director of Mixed Company theater and a clinical psychologist in private practice. She is the author of more than fifty published poems and stories, and seven produced plays, including "Girl Talk," co-authored with Carolyn Myers, which was published by Samuel French in 1992. §

KIRSTEN BACKSTROM teaches writing classes, makes sculptural baskets, works in bookstores, and does odd jobs to support herself, but writing is her primary commitment. She has written essays, reviews, stories, poetry, and four novels, often exploring lesbian themes. Most recently, her work has appeared in *Trivia* and *Hurricane Alice*.

THERESE BECKER's poetry has appeared in numerous literary magazines and anthologies including *Contemporary Michigan Poetry: Poems From The Third Coast, The New York Quarterly, The Beloit Poetry Journal, Woman Poet—The Midwest,* and *Witness* magazine. She has an M.F.A. in creative writing from Warren Wilson College and conducts workshops on the creative process, throughout Michigan, with students in grades two through twelve. She is a member of the National Press Photographer's Association and her essays, photography, and journalism have appeared in all the major Detroit newspapers. §

CATHERINE BOYD, a resident of Santa Rosa, California, has had short stories published in *Ridge Review* and *The Stump*. Several of her feature articles have appeared in the Marin/Sonoma section of the *San Francisco Examiner*, one of the city's leading newspapers. §

DOROTHY HOWE BROOKS is a former data processing consultant who writes poetry and short fiction. Her work has appeared in *Slant, Dreams and Visions, RE Arts and Letters (REAL),* and *The Georgia Journal*. She lives in Atlanta with her husband and their two sons.

STEPHANY BROWN's work has appeared in *The Short Story Review* and in *Other Voices*. She lives in Flagstaff, Arizona, with her husband and three daughters.

LORI BURKHALTER-LACKEY was born and educated in Los Angeles, California, completing her photographic training at Otis/Parsons Art Institute. Her photography has been exhibited in many California galleries and has been featured in numerous Papier-Mache Press books, including *When I Am an Old Woman I Shall Wear Purple*. Lori lives in Los Angeles with her husband, David, and their three cats. §

GRACE BUTCHER has taught English for twenty-five years at the Geauga Campus of Kent State University in Burton, Ohio. She is a life-long runner, former U.S. half-mile champion and many times Masters age group champion. She is also a motorcyclist and former columnist for *Rider* magazine. Her newest book is *Child, House, World* (Hiram Poetry Review, 1991). §

ELEANOR BYERS lives in Coeur D'Alene, Idaho, where she is active in the local chapter of the Idaho Writers League. Her poetry has appeared in *Crab Creek Review, West/Word,* and *The Seattle Times/Post Intelligencer*. She has a B.S. degree from Washington State University and lived in northern Europe for fifteen years.

LIZABETH CARPENTER, raised at the confluence of the Iowa, South Dakota, and Nebraska river borders, received an M.F.A. in 1990 from the Iowa Writers Workshop. She has published work in *The Iowa Review* and in the 1992 Eve of Saint Agnes awards issue of *Negative Capability*.

ELLIN CARTER has retired from teaching and is free-lancing. Her poems have recently appeared in *Kalliope, The G.W. Review,* and *Earth's Daughters*; also in a chapbook, *What This I And Why*, from Richmond Waters Press. §

JANET CARNCROSS CHANDLER, eighty-two, lives in a Sacramento retirement community. She is the mother of two, David and Dan, and the grandmother of two, William and Sasha. She holds an M.S.W. and was a social worker for thirty years. Now a poet for eighteen years, she has self-published three chapbooks and published *Flight of the Wild Goose* (Papier-Mache Press, 1989). Her newest book, *I Sing*, will be published by Papier-Mache Press in 1993. §

JOAN CONNOR has published more than forty stories in various anthologies and journals, including *Blueline, The Worcester Review, Re: Artes Liberales,* and *The Bridge*. She is currently working on her first novel begun on a fellowship at the MacDowell Colony.

MARIL CRABTREE lives in Kansas City, Missouri, where she weaves together a life as writer (of poetry, fiction, articles, and reviews), mediator (of domestic, interpersonal, and business conflicts), and happily married woman. Her work has appeared in *Daughters of Sarah, The Sun Magazine, Wildfire,* and other journals.

RUTH DAIGON is editor of *Poets On:*. Her latest book is *A Portable Past* (Realities Library Contemporary Poets Series, San Jose, 1987). Her poems appear in *Shenandoah, Poet Lore,* and *Kansas Quarterly*. She has published and performed her poetry in the U.S., Canada, England, and Israel and was a finalist in the Helicon Nine, Marianne Moore Poetry Contest. A professional singer, she was formerly a soprano with the New York Pro Musica, Columbia Recordings, CBS TV.

SUSAN EISENBERG is a Boston-based writer, union electrician, teacher, and activist, examining her choices. Author of the poetry book, *It's a Good Thing I'm Not Macho*, she directs the Tradeswomen Research and Education Project, gathering stories and wisdom from tradeswomen pioneers. §

SUE SANIEL ELKIND is a lifelong resident of Pittsburgh, Pennsylvania. She began writing at the age of 64 and has since published five collections—*No Longer Afraid* (Lintel, 1985), *Waiting for Order* (Naked Man Press, 1988), *Another Language* (Papier-Mache Press, 1988), *Dinosaurs and Grandparents* (MAF Press, 1988), and *Bare As the Trees* (Papier-Mache Press, 1992). She also founded and runs the Squirrel Hill Poetry Workshop in Pittsburgh. §

KAREN ETHELSDATTAR's poems and liturgies, including interfaith celebrations, affirm women and the feminine presence of God. She is co-founder of a women's ritual group, Eve's Well. Her poems have appeared in *Woman Spirit; Off Our Backs; New Women, New Church*; and in Starhawk's *The Spiral Dance*. Her name is taken to honor her mother.

MIDGE FARMER was raised in Denver and accidentally, through marriage, came "home" to Wyoming in 1959. She worked twenty-two years as a cattle rancher and now lives in Gillette where she is a house slave/writer. Her work has appeared in *Wordweavers, This Is Wyoming-Listen*, and the *Casper Arts Edition*.

RINA FERRARELLI is author of *Dreamsearch*, a chapbook of original poems (Malafemmina Press, 1992) and *Light Without Motion*, translations of poems by Giorgio Chiesura from the Italian (Owl Creek Press, 1989). She was awarded an NEA and the Italo Calvino Award. §

ALICE FRIMAN is a poet and a professor of English and creative writing at The University of Indianapolis. She has been published in journals such as *Poetry, Shenandoah, Prairie Schooner*, and *Poetry Northwest*. She is the author of five collections of poetry and the winner of the Consuelo Ford Award, 1988, and the Cecil Hemley Memorial Award, 1990, from The Poetry Society of America. Her new manuscript, *Inverted Fire*, is looking for a publisher.

MARIANNE GONTARZ is a social worker and a professional photographer, combining her work in such photography projects as the Boston Women's Health Collective *Ourselves Growing Older*. Her photographs illustrate a number of professional books and journals in the field of aging, including *A Consumer's Guide to Aging* (The Johns Hopkins University Press, 1992). She lives and works in Marin County, California. §

MAGGI ANN GRACE is a poet and fiction writer who holds an M.F.A. in Creative Writing from the University of North Carolina at Greensboro. She teaches writing to students of all ages, from public school children to women in domestic violence shelters. She lives in Durham, North Carolina, and is at work on her first novel.

NAN HUNT's explorations of dreams and other resources from the unconscious influence her poetry, essays, and fiction. She teaches in UCLA Extension's Writers' Program, lecturing widely on psychological approaches to creative processes. Her work appears in *Between Ourselves* (Houghton Mifflin), *Dreamworks, To Be A Woman* (Tarcher), and *Psychological Perspectives*.

RUTH HARRIET JACOBS, Ph.D., a sociologist and gerontologist at the Wellesley College Center for Research on Women, Wellesley, Massachusetts, authored *Be An Outrageous Older Woman* and *We Speak for Peach: An Anthology* (K.I.T. Press). Family Service America published her leaders' manual, *Older Women Surviving and Thriving*. §

TERRI L. JEWELL is a Black lesbian feminist poet/writer living in Lansing, Michigan. Her book *The Black Woman's GUMBO YA-YA: Quotations and Other Words* will be published by The Crossing Press in late 1993. Her work can be found in *African American Review, Sinister Wisdom, The Black Scholar*, and several other feminist anthologies. §

MARTHA B. JORDAN was born and raised in Mexico City. She is a founder of the multicultural Tramonane Poetry Group. Her translations and poetry have appeared in journals such as *Revista RyD* and *Manoa*. In 1987, she received the Henry M. Austin Award for Poetry from St. John's College (Annapolis/Santa Fe).

LINDA KEEGAN writes from McMurray, Pennsylvania. Originally from New Hampshire, she has worked as a journalist and paramedic. She is primarily a poet and her first chapbook, *Greedy for Sunlight*, will be published in the fall of 1992.

JUDE KEITH has been working in photography since 1978. She believes that you do not "take" pictures, but "make" them with the cooperation of light, the elements, and the subjects. Potentially the most literal art form, photography is inherently manipulation—casting a peephole for others into a world made of light, full of depth and shadows.

ALISON KOLODINSKY lives in Ormond Beach, Florida, and is a recipient of an Individual Artist Fellowship from the Florida Arts Council. She has a masters degree in clinical psychology but recently closed her private practice in order to write full time. Her work has appeared in *Poetry, Kansas Quarterly, Kalliope, JAMA*, and other publications.

ELLEN KORT, a free-lance writer, poet, and playwright from Appleton, Wisconsin, has garnered several awards for her work including Nimrod's Ruth G. Hardman/Pablo Neruda Prize For Poetry, co-sponsored by the Arts/Humanities Council of Tulsa, Oklahoma. Ellen has traveled the U.S., Australia, New Zealand, and the Bahamas to present poetry readings, Discovery Writing, Inner Awareness, and Mask-Making workshops.

LYNN KOZMA, a retired registered nurse, served in World War II. She is the author of one book of poetry, *Catching the Light* (Pocahontas Press, 1989). She has been published often by *Midwest Poetry Review, Bitterroot, Long Island Quarterly*, and *The Lyric*. She is an avid reader, gardener, and birder. A continuing student at Suffolk Community College, she is a member of Poets & Writers, Inc. §

JENNIFER LAGIER is a political activist working with the Regional Alliance for Progressive Policy. Her publication credits include *When I Am an Old Woman I Shall Wear Purple; The Dream Book: An Anthology of Writings by Italian-American Women; College English;* and *La Bella Figura*, among others. §

TRICIA LANDE is a native Californian, born in San Pedro and raised in Torrance. She has a masters degree in experimental psychology and a minor in Asian-American studies. Her short story, "Better Man," was just released in the anthology *A Loving Voice*. She is the 1992 recipient of the Marc A. Klein Playwright Award.

JANICE LEVY lives with her husband and two children in Merrick, New York. Her work has appeared in the anthologies, *Lovers* and *The Time of Our Lives*; literary magazines such as *The Sun, Prism International*, and *Buffalo Spree*; and several children's publications. She is the recipient of the *Painted Hills Review 1992* First Place Fiction Award.

BARBARA LUCAS is an associate professor of English at Nassau Community College, editor of *Xanadu*, and director of the Poetry Society of America on Long Island. Her work has appeared in *Beloit Poetry Journal, Kansas Quarterly, Birmingham Review, Slant*, and other journals.

DORIS VANDERLIPP MANLEY wrote "Good Intentions" during her years of being Superwoman. All the while, she could see the daisy field far off in the distance. Now retired, she lives happily in her little house—picking daisies as often as she wants to. §

JOANNE MCCARTHY's poetry appears in little magazines and anthologies, and in her collection *Shadowlight* (Broken Moon Press). She has published articles in *American Women Writers* and other reference works, and teaches English and creative writing at Tacoma Community College. In 1984 she spent a year in Germany on a Fulbright exchange.

SHIRLEY VOGLER MEISTER, an Indianapolis free-lance writer, has had columns, features, reviews, and poetry accepted by diverse U.S. and Canadian markets. She has earned awards for poetry, literary criticism, and journalism. Her poem, "The Coming of Winter," appeared in *When I Am an Old Woman I Shall Wear Purple*. §

ANN MENEBROKER was born in Washington, D.C., and has lived in Sacramento for forty years. She is an assistant at an art gallery and on the board of the Sacramento Poetry Center. Her most recently published collections include *Routines That Will Kill You* (BOGG Press, 1990) and *Mailbox Boogie, A Dialogue Through The Mails* (Zerx Press, 1991), with Kell Robertson.

BONNIE MICHAEL is a free-lance writer and poet living in Winston-Salem, North Carolina. She has published in major magazines, literary journals, and ten anthologies. She enjoys writing about women's and spiritual issues and travel, and reading for public radio. In her next life she plans to be a dancer. §

LILLIAN MORRISON is the author of seven collections of her own poems, most recently *Whistling the Morning In*; three anthologies of poems on sports and rhythm; and six collections of folk rhymes for children. Recent poems appear in *Aethlon, Light, Poets On*, and various anthologies. §

LESLÉA NEWMAN is the author of twelve books for adults and children including a novel, *In Every Laugh A Tear*; a poetry collection, *Sweet Dark Places*; and a book of short stories, *A Letter to Harvey Milk*. In 1989, she was awarded the prestigious Massachusetts Artists Fellowship in Poetry. §

LESLIE NYMAN, a resident of western Massachusetts, has been working as a registered nurse for fifteen years. She has been published in professional literature and is a member of her Health Maintenance Organization's ethics committee. She has been writing short fiction since obtaining a B.A. in English more than twenty years ago.

GAILMARIE PAHMEIER teaches creative writing and literature at the University of Nevada. She twice received a Nevada State Council on the Arts fellowship in literature, most recently for 1992-1993. She has published widely, and a collection of her work, *With Respect for Distance*, is forthcoming from Black Rock Press.

NITA PENFOLD struggles to write while filling her "empty nest" with deferred dreams. Her poetry has appeared in the anthologies *Cries of the Spirit* (Beacon Press), *Catholic Girls* (Penguin Books), and in over forty small press magazines including *Earth's Daughters* and the *Maryland Review*.

FRAN PORTLEY majored in English Honors at Duke University. She teaches poetry to children in the New Jersey JOY (joining old and young) program. Her poems have appeared in *When I Am an Old Woman I Shall Wear Purple, Parting Gifts, Heartland, Stone Country*, and many other publications. §

JACKLYN W. POTTER has published work in journals such as *Stone Country Journal* and *The Washington Review*, and will be in a forthcoming anthology of *Poets on the Air*, WPFW-FM radio. She directs the Miller Cabin Poetry Series and is president of The Poetry Committee of Greater Washington, D.C. Area. She teaches creative writing in College Park, Maryland. §

SANDRA REDDING, at fifty, received an M.F.A. in Creative Writing from the University of North Carolina-Greensboro. She now teaches creative writing courses at Guilford Technical Community College and at the Presbyterian Home in High Point, North Carolina. Short story publications in 1992 include *Crucible* and *The Nightshade Short Story Reader*. §

ELISAVIETTA RITCHIE's *Flying Time: Stories & Half-Stories* includes four PEN Syndicated Fiction Project winners. *Tightening The Circle Over Eel Country* won the 1975-76 Great Lakes Colleges Association's "New Writer's Prize for Best First Book of Poetry," and *Raking The Snow* won the 1981 Washington Writer's Publishing House competition. Editor of *The Dolphin's Arc: Poems on Endangered Creatures of the Sea* and other books, she has read at the Library of Congress and many other venues in the U.S., Brazil, the Far East, the Balkans, and Canada. She lives in Washington, D.C. and Toronto. §

ELAINE ROTHMAN moved to rural Connecticut after twenty years of teaching and counseling in urban and suburban schools. She learned about her new community through writing feature stories for local newspapers. Five years and two hundred articles later, she left journalism for a writers' course at the University of Iowa's Elderhostel program, and has written fiction ever since.

LORI RUSSELL is a free-lance writer and part-time home health nurse. Her short stories and poetry have appeared in *Milvia Street* and *Fire Folio*. A twenty-eight-year resident of the San Francisco Bay Area, Lori and her husband have recently relocated to The Dalles, Oregon.

PAT SCHNEIDER has published poetry, fiction, plays, and libretti. She is founder/director of Amherst Writers & Artists and AWA Press. *The Writer Alone & With Others* (working title) is forthcoming from Lowell House; *Tell Me Something I Can't Forget* is available from four-time Academy Award nominee Florentine Films.

CAROL SCHWALBERG is a hyphenate (author-journalist-critic-photographer-editor-university lecturer) whose short stories have appeared in *Ita* and *Fair Lady* and whose poems have run in *West* and *Black River Review*. She is neutral on the subject of cauliflower.

JAN EPTON SEALE is a native Texan. She is the author of two books of poetry and a new collection of short stories, *Airlift* (T.C.U. Press). Seven of her stories have appeared in the PEN Syndicated Fiction Project.

BETTIE M. SELLERS is a Goolsby Professor of English at Young Harris College, Georgia. She is the author of several collections of poems—*Spring Onions and Cornbread, Liza's Monday, Morning of the Red-Tailed Hawk*, and *Wild Ginger*—and has produced a documentary film, *The Bitter Berry: The Life and Works of Byron Herbert Reece* (1988 Georgia Emmy). In 1992 she wrote a resource manual, *The Bitter Berry*. §

JOANNE SELTZER has published hundreds of poems in literary magazines, newspapers, and anthologies, including *When I Am an Old Woman I Shall Wear Purple, The Tie That Binds*, and *If I Had a Hammer*. She has also published short fiction, non-fiction prose, translations of French poetry, and three poetry chapbooks. §

ENID SHOMER's award-winning stories and poems have appeared in *The New Yorker, The Paris Review*, and other journals. Her new books are *This Close to the Earth: Poems* (University of Arkansas Press, 1992) and *Imaginary Men*, a book of stories which won the Iowa Short Fiction Award and will appear in 1993. §

LINDA WASMER SMITH, a free-lance medical journalist, grew up on an Arkansas farm. She now lives in Albuquerque, New Mexico, with her husband and their two children. Her poetry has appeared recently in many literary magazines, including *Plains Poetry Journal* and *Light*. Her more than four hundred articles on health and medicine have been published in numerous national periodicals, including *American Health* and *Outdoor Life*.

NADINE STAIR is attributed with writing "If I Had My Life to Live Over I Would Pick More Daisies" at the age of eighty-five. She is believed to have been living in Kentucky at that time. Papier-Mache Press has been unable to contact a living relative to learn more about her poetry.

RANDEANE TETU has received several national awards for fiction. "Depth of Field" is listed in *The Best American Short Stories, 1989*. Her work has appeared in many magazines and anthologies, including the 1991 American Booksellers Association Honors Book, *When I Am an Old Woman I Shall Wear Purple* (Papier-Mache Press, 1987). §

BARBARA L. THOMAS began writing poetry after turning sixty. She has been published in *Raven's Chronicles, Upstream, Spindrift, Chrysanthemum*, and other journals. A long-distance swimmer in the cold, Pacific Northwest waters, she is a daughter of living parents born in the nineteenth century, a Shawnee granddaughter, a calligrapher, and a member of a small performance group, The Avalanche Poets. §

ANNA TOMCZAK has an M.F.A. in Fine Art Photography from the University of Florida. She has received numerous grants and awards, including an NEA/SECCA Southeast Seven Artist Fellowship and an Atlantic Center for the Arts Cultural Exchange Fellowship to La Napoule Art Foundation, France. Her work has been exhibited internationally in galleries and museums and is represented in several private, corporate, and museum collections.

CLAUDIA VAN GERVEN lives in Boulder, Colorado, where she has taught writing classes for the past fifteen years. She has been published in many magazines including *Prairie Schooner, Calyx*, and *Frontiers*. Her work will be appearing in three forthcoming anthologies.

SUSAN VREELAND received First Place in Short Fiction in the 1991 California Writers' Roundtable sponsored by the Women's National Book Association. Her short stories appeared in *Crosscurrents* and *Ambergris*, and her travel writing appeared in *Travel and Leisure* and *Los Angeles Times*. She is working on a novel about Canadian artist Emily Carr.

KENNETTE H. WILKES is an individual artist on the Alabama State Council on the Arts with an M.A. in creative studies. She has had reviews, interviews, and a novel excerpt published. Her poetry has been published in *Nimrod, Negative Capability, Green Fuse*, and the *Journal of Poetry Therapy*. First prize winner of the Oklahoma Collegiate Poet and Alabama State literary competitions in essay, one-act play, and contemporary poem. She currently has a trilogy of historical novels in progress.

§ Denotes contributors whose work has appeared in previous Papier-Mache Press anthologies.

Quality Books from Papier-Mache Press

At Papier-Mache Press our goal is to produce attractive, accessible books that deal with contemporary personal, social, and political issues. Our titles have found an enthusiastic audience in general interest, women's, new age, and Christian bookstores, as well as gift stores, mail order catalogs, and libraries. Many have also been used by teachers for women's studies, creative writing and gerontology classes, and by therapists and family counselors to help clients explore personal issues such as aging and relationships.

If you are interested in finding out more about our other titles, ask your local bookstores which Papier-Mache items they carry. Or, if you would like to receive a complete catalog of books, posters, shirts, and postcards from Papier-Mache Press, please send a self-addressed stamped envelope to:

Papier-Mache Press
PO Box 1304
Freedom, CA 95019